Quilts of Cumberland County

LETORT QUILTERS DOCUMENTATION PROJECT

4880 Lower Valley Road • Atglen, PA 19310

Other Schiffer Books on Related Subjects:

Quilts: The Fabric of Friendship, York County Quilt Documentation Project, 978-0-7643-1195-6
Quilts of Virginia 1607-1899: The Birth of America Through the Eye of a Needle,
      Virginia Consortium of Quilters' Documentation Project, 978-0-7643-2465-9
Quilting Traditions: Pieces from the Past, Patricia T. Herr, 978-0-7643-1121-5
Quilts and Quiltmakers Covering Connecticut, Connecticut Quilt Search Project, 978-0-7643-1472-8

Published by Schiffer Publishing, Ltd.
4880 Lower Valley Road
Atglen, PA 19310
Phone: (610) 593-1777; Fax: (610) 593-2002
E-mail: Info@schifferbooks.com
Web: www.schifferbooks.com

Library of Congress Control Number: 2016930713

Designed by RoS
Cover design by Brenda McCallum
Type set in Goudy Old Style
ISBN: 978-0-7643-5109-9
Printed in China

For our complete selection of fine books on this and related subjects, please visit our website at www.
schifferbooks.com. You may also write for a free catalog.

Schiffer Publishing's titles are available at special discounts for bulk purchases for sales promotions or
premiums. Special editions, including personalized covers, corporate imprints, and excerpts, can be
created in large quantities for special needs. For more information, contact the publisher.

We are always looking for people to write books on new and related subjects. If you have an idea for a
book, please contact us at proposals@schifferbooks.com.

Contents

Preface

When a few members of the LeTort Quilters decided to do a quilt documentation project in Cumberland County, we were following a tradition of documenting this heritage of work by women. Other states and a number of our neighboring counties documented their quilts decades ahead of us, so we had the opportunity to learn from others.

Most of us didn't know much about vintage quilts when we started out. We were quilters first and learned a lot along the way. This book is designed for others like us who find quilts to be a source of comfort, beauty, and intriguing history. We hope that it will inspire you to look at quilts more closely and to value some of those old, lost treasures you may come across in attics, family blanket chests, garage sales, or flea markets.

The documentation project ran from 2011 through 2014. We elected to document all vintage quilts (quilts completed before 1970) residing in Cumberland County during that time. Documentation days were held at various locations throughout the county. To bring in quilt owners, we spread the word of our efforts in a variety of ways and received some excellent coverage in the local news media. Although we documented over 900 quilts, we know we didn't get them all, so there will always be room for follow-up documentations.

We had thought that in the end, we would have a clear picture of the typical Cumberland County quilt, but that didn't happen. What we did find were some unexpected aspects of quilt history that we now think may be representative of quilts today. First, many quilts were in the hands of family members where they were being cherished and handed down through generations. However, few of these quilts actually originated in Cumberland County. People move, and their quilts and quilt history move with them. Cumberland County, a crossroads community since its inception, reflects that fluidity perhaps more than some other regions.

Second, quite a number of quilt collectors in our county had scores, and even hundreds, of quilts in their possession. Their quilts were purchased locally at public auctions and estate sales, flea markets, antique shops throughout the United States, and even in other countries. Frequently these collectors knew nothing of the history of their quilts, but had at least saved them from a dumpster. Sometimes what appears to be documentation about a quilt's history turns out to be incorrect. Names and initials on a quilt may not be those of the maker and even dates may not accurately reflect when a quilt was completed. Family stories often turn out to be incorrect, as when the fabrics can be dated to a time period well after the supposed quilt maker lived. These things add to the intrigue and can lead to an interesting lesson in history.

All of these quilts have now been documented, and their photos and available history are now at the Cumberland County Historical Society. The movement of these quilts has continued. Some of the quilts have been donated to museums or sent to family members in other parts of the country, and still others have been sold to collectors in other states.

The book is organized to give an overview of our findings. We start with a short history of Cumberland County, and then share a story of the travels of a typical quilt. That is followed by a photo gallery of quilts found during the documentation, organized by basic construction or type of quilt with some history where available. We think this will give a fairly extensive overview of vintage quilts in general—our own crossroads of quilts. Finally, we offer tips on finding and caring for vintage quilts. We hope this whets your appetite for an important part of our heritage and gives you some tools for rescuing and caring for the quilts that come into your life.

Acknowledgments

This book is the product of a dedicated team effort. Those of us on the Cumberland County Quilt Documentation Steering Committee found ourselves part of a small and efficient team of women who shared their expertise, energy, and time in much the way that a great relay team works. The decision to document all quilts residing in Cumberland County was recognized to be a huge task and planned for accordingly. Documentation days were organized throughout the county, advertised well, and staffed with an army of volunteers. A database was created to house all the information, and we managed to document over 900 quilts, as well as produce a book that shares our findings with others.

We want to acknowledge the support of the Franklin County Documentation Project for providing incentive and seed money for the project and to the entire membership of the LeTort Quilters who embraced and encouraged this multi-year project. Further thanks go to the Cumberland County Historical Society, our partner in this endeavor, where the final database will be housed and made available to anyone interested in knowing more about the quilts we saw.

Thanks are due to Bethany Village, Mechanicsburg; Christ United Methodist Church, Shippensburg; Green Ridge Retirement Village, Newville; Messiah Village, Mechanicsburg; Mt. Zion United Methodist Church, Enola; St. Stephen Lutheran Church, New Kingstown; and Trindle Spring Lutheran Church, Mechanicsburg, for allowing days of documentation in their facilities.

The following volunteers gave of their time to document, photograph, and otherwise support this project. None of this would have been possible without their commitment of time, sense of history, and openness to learning along the way:

Susan Aigeldinger, Ginny Aires, Beth Bacher, Jennifer Betar, Anna Beckley, Jane Black, Alice Boose, Karen K. Buckley, Ann Burke, Stacy Clady, Deb Cooney, Susan DeIorio, Laura Dries, Jan Fitch, Barbara Garrett, Betsy Golden, Sandra Harmon, Dawn Heefner, Susan Horner, Trish Herr, Val Johnson, Katha Kierit, Patsy Kiner, Susan Kline, Martha Knox, Jacqueline Kreitzer, Tammy Long, Jazmyne Markham, Lytle Markham, Cindy Mentzer, Barbara Miller, Mim Miller, Joyce Moyer, Lois Muzzy, Janet Nelson, Barbara Nickle, Sharon Pinka, Karen Pinker, Adele Rall, Evelyn Rebenstorff, Carolyn Rutherford, Susan Rynex, Linda Stoltz, Merrill Thrush, Richard Tritt, Sarah R. Wannamaker, Cathie Walker, Shirley Walker, Diane Watkins, Rita Wilson, and Rachel Zuch.

Thanks to all of you from the Cumberland County Quilt Documentation Committee: Martha Jones, Lin Keller, Elizabeth Kisielewski, Debra Lohman, Donna Lohman, Barbara Myers, and Barbara A. Thrush.

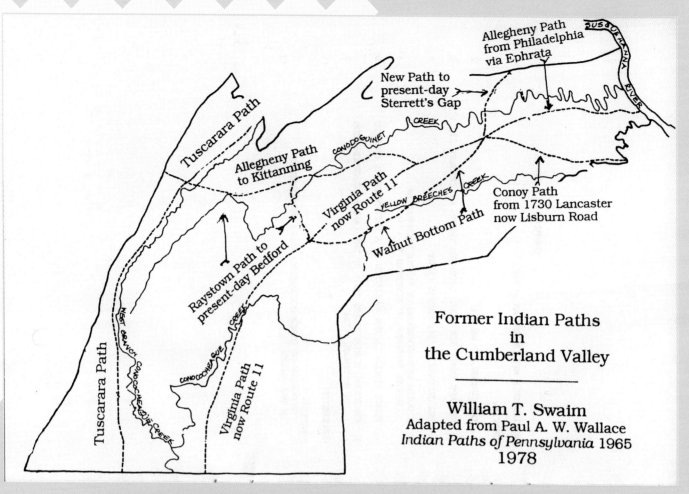

Tuscarara Path

Allegheny Path from Philadelphia via Ephrata

New Path to present-day Sterrett's Gap

CREEK

SUSQUEHANNA RIVER

CONODOGUINET

Allegheny Path to Kittanning

Virginia Path now Route 11

YELLOW BREECHES CREEK

Conoy Path from 1730 Lancaster now Lisburn Road

Raystown Path to present-day Bedford

Walnut Bottom Path

WEST BRANCH CONOCOCHEAGUE CREEK

CONOCOCHEAGUE CREEK

Tuscarara Path

Virginia Path now Route 11

Former Indian Paths in the Cumberland Valley

William T. Swaim
Adapted from Paul A. W. Wallace
Indian Paths of Pennsylvania 1965
1978

"Former Indian Paths in the Cumberland Valley," 1978 drawing by William T. Swaim, adapted from *Indian Paths of Pennsylvania*, Paul A. W. Wallace. *Courtesy of the Cumberland County Historical Society*

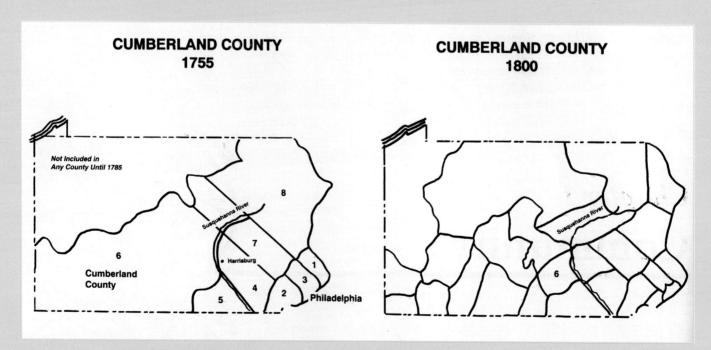

CUMBERLAND COUNTY 1755

Not Included in Any County Until 1785

Cumberland County

Susquehanna River

Harrisburg

6

8

7

1

4

2

3

5

Philadelphia

CUMBERLAND COUNTY 1800

Susquehanna River

6

Maps of Cumberland County in 1755 and 1800 comparing the land area of the county. *Cloth and Costume 1750–1880*, Tandy and Charles Hersh. *Courtesy of the Cumberland County Historical Society*

Introduction

Cumberland County is on the western side of the Susquehanna River, directly across from the Pennsylvania state capital, Harrisburg. Encompassing approximately 500 square miles, it has a rich tradition of education, a diverse economic base, and has always been recognized as a key transportation hub. Cumberland County has deep historical roots in our country's development and has been a leader in preserving much of that history for posterity.

Until 1720, the area that became Cumberland County was Indian land. Even then it was a major transportation route with a number of major Indian paths that have evolved into interstate highways. As early as 1733, James LeTort, Peter Chartier, and George Croghan were successful traders in the area, and settlers had begun to arrive and establish small settlements as far west as Shippensburg. In 1750, Cumberland County was legally formed by William Penn, his family, and Pennsylvania's General Assembly. In its original configuration, the county covered all of the land west of the Susquehanna and north of York County. Cumberland was the sixth county established in Pennsylvania and the second west of the Susquehanna. It was created to help control the western expansion of Europeans into the country's interior, serving as the legal center for all settlers from the Susquehanna to the Ohio Rivers.

As settlements increased, the original area of Cumberland was divided into smaller counties. By 1800, the counties of Bedford, Blair, Centre, Fulton, Huntingdon, Juniata, Mifflin, and Perry were created out of what had once been Cumberland. However, its central function as a legal and transportation hub has continued to influence the development of the county.

The French and Indian campaigns during the mid-1700s influenced the establishment of forts and military supply routes in the county. The Revolutionary War built on these routes, with the army barracks in Carlisle serving the War for Independence. These barracks were burned to the ground in 1863 by Lieutenant General Richard Ewell, as his division of Lee's Army of Northern Virginia led troops into this northernmost intrusion of the Confederacy during the Civil War. The Carlisle barracks also served as the location of the Carlisle Indian School, established in 1879 by the Indian Bureau of the Interior until its closure in 1918. Currently the site of the Army War College, this site has had an ongoing role in every United States conflict since its inception.

Map by Paul J. Connor showing Pennsylvania counties in 1770. *Mother Cumberland*, Raymond M. Bell. *Courtesy of the Cumberland County Historical Society*

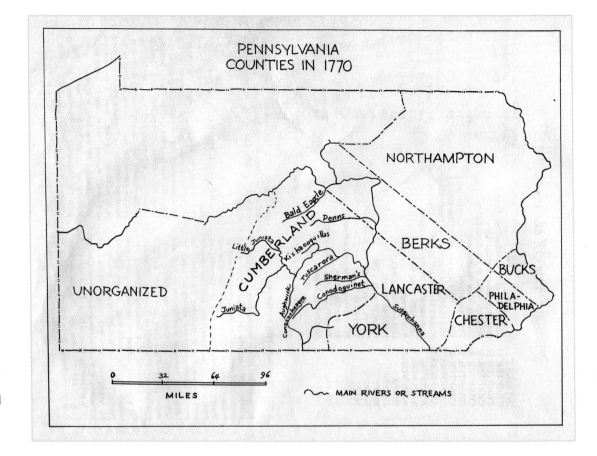

PENNSYLVANIA COUNTIES IN 1770

NORTHAMPTON

BERKS

BUCKS

LANCASTER

PHILA-DELPHIA

CHESTER

YORK

CUMBERLAND

UNORGANIZED

Bald Eagle

Penns

Juniata

Little

Kishacoquillas

Tuscarora

Sherman's

Conodoquinet

Aughwick

Conococheague

Susquehanna

Juniata

0   32   64   96
MILES

∿∿∿ MAIN RIVERS OR STREAMS

Map by John D. Hemminger showing public roads laid out through Cumberland County prior to 1800. *Courtesy of Cumberland County Historical Society*

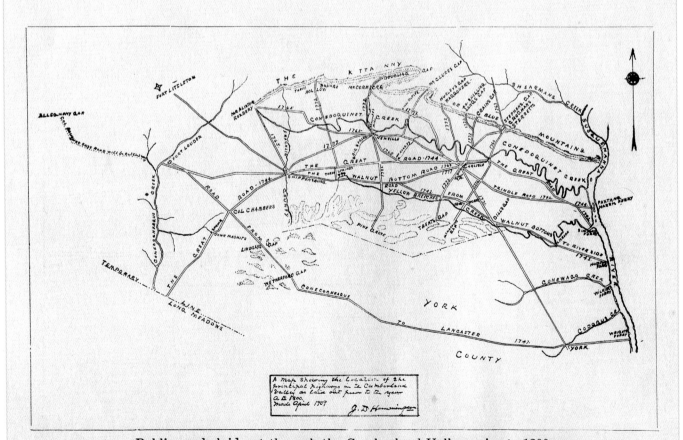

Public roads laid out through the Cumberland Valley prior to 1800.

Hessian guard house, c. 1890, on the grounds of the Carlisle Indian School. The structure was built by Hessian prisoners in 1777. Photo by John N. Choate. *Courtesy of the Cumberland County Historical Society*

Cumberland County has a long history of commitment to education. Dickinson College was established in the late 1760s and continues to function as a well-respected liberal arts college. The Dickinson School of Law (unrelated to the college) was established in 1834 by Judge John Reed and has been the school of countless leaders in Pennsylvania and US history. The law school is now part of Penn State University. The Irving Female College, established in Mechanicsburg in 1856, was one of the first colleges for women. Currently, Cumberland County is home to six colleges and universities.

Cumberland County also boasts a strong and diverse economy. From its earliest days, the county maintained a wide range of occupations and social statuses. Early settlements included farmers who produced a variety of products for both local use and trade. The county's position as a gateway west and south enhanced the opportunities for trade. During the nineteenth century, there was a period of iron production, and in the early to mid-twentieth century, a "golden age" of light manufacturing. According to one writer, "Ingenuity was characteristic of the golden age of light manufacturing. The Carlisle Garment Company, a spin-off of the J. W. Plank Department Store, claimed to have produced the first ready-to-wear women's clothing in 1890, motivated by a need to keep department store workers busy in the slack winter season" (Louise M. Waddell, "Courageous Cumberland County," *Pennsylvania Heritage*, a quarterly publication of the Pennsylvania Historical and Museum Commission, vol. 7, no. 3, Summer 1991, page 10).

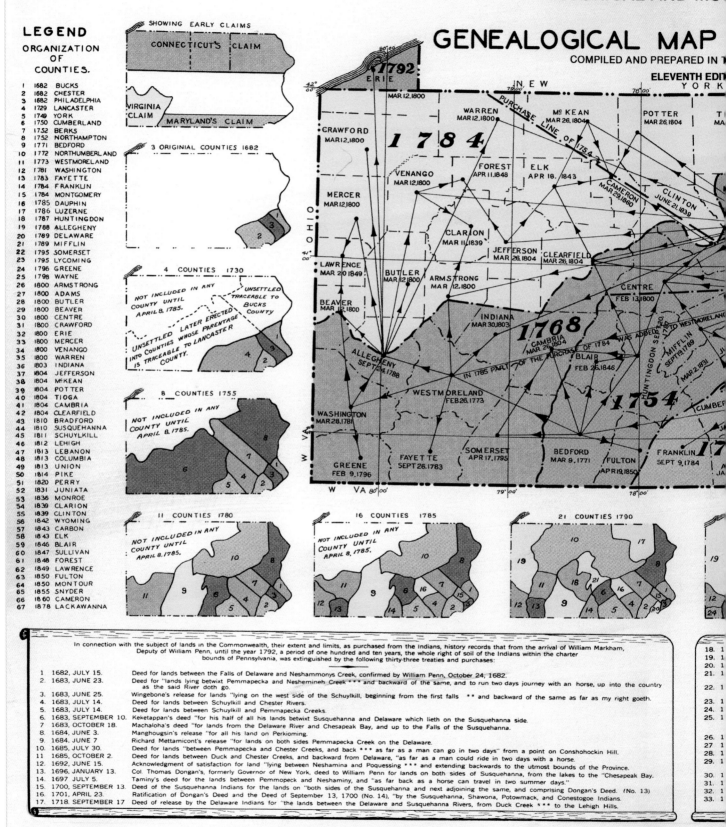

COMMONWEALTH O...

HISTORICAL AND MUS...

GENEALOGICAL MAP

COMPILED AND PREPARED IN T...

ELEVENTH EDIT...
YORK...

LEGEND

ORGANIZATION OF COUNTIES.

1	1682	BUCKS
2	1682	CHESTER
3	1682	PHILADELPHIA
4	1729	LANCASTER
5	1749	YORK
6	1750	CUMBERLAND
7	1752	BERKS
8	1752	NORTHAMPTON
9	1771	BEDFORD
10	1772	NORTHUMBERLAND
11	1773	WESTMORELAND
12	1781	WASHINGTON
13	1783	FAYETTE
14	1784	FRANKLIN
15	1784	MONTGOMERY
16	1785	DAUPHIN
17	1786	LUZERNE
18	1787	HUNTINGDON
19	1788	ALLEGHENY
20	1789	DELAWARE
21	1789	MIFFLIN
22	1795	SOMERSET
23	1795	LYCOMING
24	1796	GREENE
25	1798	WAYNE
26	1800	ARMSTRONG
27	1800	ADAMS
28	1800	BUTLER
29	1800	BEAVER
30	1800	CENTRE
31	1800	CRAWFORD
32	1800	ERIE
33	1800	MERCER
34	1800	VENANGO
35	1800	WARREN
36	1803	INDIANA
37	1804	JEFFERSON
38	1804	McKEAN
39	1804	POTTER
40	1804	TIOGA
41	1804	CAMBRIA
42	1804	CLEARFIELD
43	1810	BRADFORD
44	1810	SUSQUEHANNA
45	1811	SCHUYLKILL
46	1812	LEHIGH
47	1813	LEBANON
48	1813	COLUMBIA
49	1813	UNION
50	1814	PIKE
51	1820	PERRY
52	1831	JUNIATA
53	1836	MONROE
54	1839	CLARION
55	1839	CLINTON
56	1842	WYOMING
57	1843	CARBON
58	1843	ELK
59	1846	BLAIR
60	1847	SULLIVAN
61	1848	FOREST
62	1849	LAWRENCE
63	1850	FULTON
64	1850	MONTOUR
65	1855	SNYDER
66	1860	CAMERON
67	1878	LACKAWANNA

SHOWING EARLY CLAIMS

CONNECTICUT'S CLAIM

VIRGINIA CLAIM

MARYLAND'S CLAIM

3 ORIGINAL COUNTIES 1682

4 COUNTIES 1730

NOT INCLUDED IN ANY COUNTY UNTIL APRIL 8, 1785.

UNSETTLED TRACEABLE TO BUCKS COUNTY

UNSETTLED LATER ERECTED INTO COUNTIES WHOSE PARENTAGE IS TRACEABLE TO LANCASTER COUNTY.

8 COUNTIES 1755

NOT INCLUDED IN ANY COUNTY UNTIL APRIL 8, 1785.

11 COUNTIES 1780

NOT INCLUDED IN ANY COUNTY UNTIL APRIL 8, 1785.

16 COUNTIES 1785

NOT INCLUDED IN ANY COUNTY UNTIL APRIL 8, 1785.

21 COUNTIES 1790

In connection with the subject of lands in the Commonwealth, their extent and limits, as purchased from the Indians, history records that from the arrival of William Markham, Deputy of William Penn, until the year 1792, a period of one hundred and ten years, the whole right of soil of the Indians within the charter bounds of Pennsylvania, was extinguished by the following thirty-three treaties and purchases.

1. 1682, JULY 15. Deed for lands between the Falls of Delaware and Neshammonys Creek, confirmed by William Penn, October 24, 1682.
2. 1683, JUNE 23. Deed for "lands lying betwixt Pemmapecka and Neshemineh Creek *** and backward of the same, and to run two days journey with an horse, up into the country as the said River doth go.
3. 1683, JUNE 25. Wingebone's release for lands "lying on the west side of the Schuylkill, beginning from the first falls ** and backward of the same as far as my right goeth.
4. 1683, JULY 14. Deed for lands between Schuylkill and Chester Rivers.
5. 1683, JULY 14. Deed for lands between Schuylkill and Pemmapecka Creeks.
6. 1683, SEPTEMBER 10. Keketappan's deed "for his half of all his lands betwixt Susquehanna and Delaware which lieth on the Susquehanna side.
7. 1683, OCTOBER 18. Machaloha's deed "for lands from the Delaware River and Chesapeak Bay, and up to the Falls of the Susquehanna.
8. 1684, JUNE 3. Manghougsin's release "for all his land on Perkioming.
9. 1684, JUNE 7. Richard Mettamicont's release "for lands on both sides Pemmapecka Creek on the Delaware.
10. 1685, JULY 30. Deed for lands "between Pemmapecka and Chester Creeks, and back *** as far as a man can go in two days" from a point on Conshohockin Hill.
11. 1685, OCTOBER 2. Deed for lands between Duck and Chester Creeks, and backward from Delaware, "as far as a man could ride in two days with a horse.
12. 1692, JUNE 15. Acknowledgment of satisfaction for land "lying between Neshamina and Poquessing *** and extending backwards to the utmost bounds of the Province.
13. 1696, JANUARY 13. Col. Thomas Dongan's, formerly Governor of New York, deed to William Penn for lands on both sides of Susquehanna, from the lakes to the "Chesapeak Bay.
14. 1697 JULY 5. Taminy's deed for the lands between Pemmopeck and Neshaminy, and "as far back as a horse can travel in two summer days."
15. 1700, SEPTEMBER 13. Deed of the Susquehanna Indians for the lands on "both sides of the Susquehanna and next adjoining the same, and comprising Dongan's Deed. (No. 13)
16. 1701, APRIL 23. Ratification of Dongan's Deed and the Deed of September 13, 1700 (No. 14), "by the Susquehanna, Shawona, Potowmack, and Conestogoe Indians.
17. 1718. SEPTEMBER 17 Deed of release by the Delaware Indians for "the lands between the Delaware and Susquehanna Rivers, from Duck Creek *** to the Lehigh Hills.

18. 1
19. 1
20. 1
21. 1
22. 1
23. 1
24. 1
25. 1
26. 1
27. 1
28. 1
29. 1
30. 1
31. 1
32. 1
33. 1

PENNSYLVANIA

M COMMISSION

THE COUNTIES

ND OFFICE 1933

99

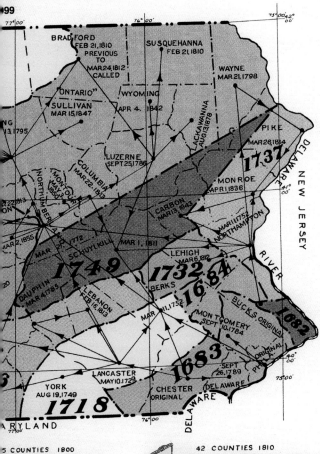

BRADFORD
FEB 21,1810
PREVIOUS
TO
MAR 24,1812
CALLED

SUSQUEHANNA
FEB 21,1810

WAYNE
MAR 21,1798

"ONTARIO"

WYOMING
APR 4, 1842

SULLIVAN
MAR 15,1847

PIKE

LACKAWANNA
AUG 13,1878

LUZERNE
SEPT 25,1786

MAR 28,1814

1737

COLUMBIA
MAR 22, 1813

MONROE
APR 1,1836

NEW JERSEY

CARBON
MAR 13, 1843

MAR 11,1752
NORTHAMPTON

SCHUYLKILL
MAR 1, 1811

LEHIGH
MAR 6,1812

1749

1732

1684

DELAWARE RIVER

DAUPHIN
MAR 4,1785

LEBANON
FEB 16,1813

BERKS

MAR 11,1752

1682

MONTGOMERY
SEPT 10,1784

BUCKS ORIGINAL

1683

LANCASTER
MAY 10,1729

YORK
AUG 19,1749

CHESTER
ORIGINAL

DELAWARE

SEPT 26,1789

ORIGINAL

1718

MARYLAND

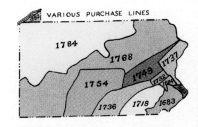

VARIOUS PURCHASE LINES

1784

1768

1737

1754

1749

1736

1718

1683

DATES OF THE VARIOUS TREATIES & PURCHASES

	FIRST PURCHASE	
	1	JULY 15 1682

6 DEEDS & RELEASES

	2	JUNE 23 1683
	3	JUNE 25 1683
	4	JULY 14 1683
	5	JULY 14 1683
	6	SEPT 10 1683
	7	OCT 18 1683

9 DEEDS & RELEASES COVERING THIS AND FORMER PURCHASES

	8	JUNE 3 1684
	9	JUNE 7 1684
	10	JULY 30 1685
	11	OCT 2 1685
	2	JUNE 15 1692
	13	JAN 3 1696
	14	JULY 5 1697
	15	SEPT 13 1700
	16	APR 23 1701

SUSQUEHANNA & DELAWARE INDIANS

	17	SEPT 17 1718
	18	DEC 16 1720
	19	MAY 31 1726

SCHUYLKILL INDIANS

	20	SEPT 7 1732

FIVE INDIAN NATIONS

	21	OCT 1 1736
	22	OCT 25 1736

WALKING PURCHASE

	23	AUG 25 1737

NINE INDIAN NATIONS

	24	AUG 22 1749

TREATY OF ALBANY

	25	JULY 6 1754
	26	OCT 23 1758

NEW PURCHASE

	27	SEPT 5 1768
	28	NOV 5 1768

LAST PURCHASE

	29	OCT 23 1784
	30	DEC 21 1784
	31	JAN 21 1785

PRESQUE ISLE

	32	JAN 9 1789
	33	MAR 3 1792

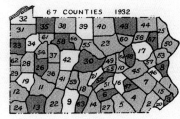

67 COUNTIES 1932

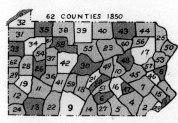

62 COUNTIES 1850

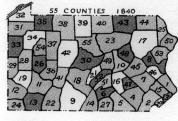

55 COUNTIES 1840

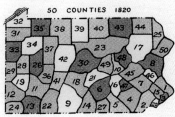

50 COUNTIES 1820

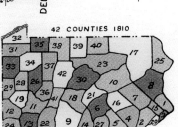

COUNTIES 1800

42 COUNTIES 1810

EMBER 16. Deed settling controversy respecting boundary of the lands arising from dispute concerning distance a man and a horse can each travel in a day.

31. Deed for lands on both sides of Brandywine Creek.

TEMBER 7 Deed for lands between "Lechay Hills and Kekachtanemin Hills, between Schuylkill and its branches, and the branches of Delaware.

OBER 11 Deed "for all the said River Susquehanna with the lands lying on both sides thereof, eastward to the head of the branches, or springs running into the Susquehanna, and westward "to the setting of the sun," and from its mouth northward "to the hills or mountains called Kekachtanemin.

OBER 25. The preceding deed declared by the Indians to include the lands on the Delaware, "and all the lands on both sides of the River Susquehanna from the mouth thereof as far northward, * * * to the ridge of Hills called Tyoninhaschta."

UST 25. Deed comprising the "Walking Purchase, or, "as far as a man can go in one day and an half" from the westerly branch of Neshamony to the Delaware.

UST 22. Deed for lands from the "Kekactany Hills to Maghonioy Mountain, and between Susquehanna and Delaware on the north side of "Lechawachsein Creek.

6. Deed at Albany for the lands on the west side of Susquehanna River, from Kittochtinny Hills to a mile above the mouth of Penn's Creek, "thence northwest and by west, as far as the Province extends to its western lines, * * * thence to the southern boundary, * * * thence by the southern boundary to the * * * Kittochtinny Hills, * * * thence by the south side of the said Hills to the Beginning."

OBER 23. Deed of surrender of part of the Purchase of 1754, and new boundaries declared and confirmed.

TEMBER 5. The end of "Nittany Mountain assumed as a station, per deed made, and surveys not usually made north thereof.

EMBER 5. Deed at Fort Stanwix, commonly called the "New Purchase, extending from northeast to southwest corner of Commonwealth.

OBER 23. Deed explaining the boundary at the treaty at Fort Stanwix and Pine Creek, declared to have been the boundary designated by the Indians, commonly called the "Last Purchase."

EMBER 21. Deed declaring Lycoming to be the boundary.

JARY 21. Deed at Fort Stanwix and Fort McIntosh for the residue of the lands within the Commonwealth, made October 23, 1784, and January 21, 1785.

JARY 9. Indian cession of lands at Presque Isle including the Triangle.

CH 3 On October 3, 1788, an Act was passed authorizing the Supreme Executive Council to draw on the State Treasurer for a sum of money for defraying the expense of purchasing from the Indians lands on Lake Erie. It is usually called the "Purchase of the Triangle. It contains 202,187 acres.

11

Other creative and innovative businesses contribute to the vibrant economy. Currently the county benefits from employment opportunities in federal, state, and county governments and from its ongoing function as a transportation and trade hub.

Cumberland County's rich history makes it a unique setting for exploring the vintage quilts in its midst. As a major crossroads from its earliest days, this south-central Pennsylvania county has been a place for people to settle from many other regions. They have brought with them quilts and quilting traditions from other parts of the state and the country. From its earliest days, there has been a large selection of textiles for household use, adding to the variety of quilts.

Carlisle Garment Company on North Bedford Street, c. 1910.
Photo by A. A. Line.
Courtesy of the Cumberland County Historical Society

Sewing room in the Carlisle Garment Company, c. 1900.
Photographer unknown. *Courtesy of the Cumberland
County Historical Society*

Preservation also has deep roots in this community. The Cumberland
County Historical Society was founded in 1874 and is among the oldest in the
nation. It has been a leader in recognizing the importance of textiles, including
quilts, as a part of our heritage. In 1985, the society produced the book *Cloth
and Costume, 1750–1850*, and has established a vintage quilt collection that is
carefully preserved and publicly displayed. There are also many private quilt
collectors in the county. Some have large collections of 100 or more; others
are simply the recognized conservator of one or more family heirloom quilts.
This book showcases that diversity. Regardless of where some quilts originated,
Cumberland County is a place where the art and craft of quilting is valued
and carefully preserved.

Old Cumberland County, Pennsylvania, courthouse tower during repairs, c. 1865. Contractor Charles Hoffer and his brother-in-law, Henry A. Crabbe, are on top of the lantern. Copied from the original carte-de-visite photo by J. C. Lesher, Carlisle. *Courtesy of Cumberland County Historical Society*

Detail of a pillar on the Old Cumberland County Courthouse showing damage from the shelling of Carlisle during the Confederate invasion on July 1, 1863. Photo by Jim Bradley, June 13, 1997. *Courtesy of the Cumberland County Historical Society*

The original entrance to the Cumberland County Historical Society, Carlisle, October 1997. *Courtesy of the Cumberland County Historical Society*

View of Two Mile House, part of the Cumberland County Historical Society and site for documentation of quilts for the Cumberland County Quilt Documentation Project 2011–2014. *Courtesy of The Cumberland County Historical Society*

Interior of History on High, the Shop. *Courtesy of Cumberland County Historical Society*

Exterior view of History on High, the Shop, at 33 W. High Street, Carlisle. The shop is part of the Cumberland County Historical Society.

Oakleaf and Tulip friendship quilt, 1856. 94" × 92". Completed by the women of Trindle Spring Lutheran Church, Mechanicsburg, Pennsylvania. Signed by all sixteen quilt makers. Quilt was purchased in Paducah, Kentucky, in 1998 and returned to the church in 2010. It is on display in a glass case at the church and cared for by the church's quilt group.

CHAPTER 1

Trindle Spring

Story of a Quilt's Travels

In the fall of 2001, members of the Trindle Spring Lutheran Church in Mechanicsburg, Pennsylvania, had a visitor. Gloria Leonard Hall, from Palmyra, Nebraska, arrived with a quilt that had been made by women at the Trindle Spring Church in 1856. She wondered if they would like to have it come home to them.

Hall was a quilt historian, appraiser, and collector who traveled worldwide lecturing about quilts and their heritage, and this quilt had been traveling the world with her since 1998. She had purchased it at a shop in Paducah, Kentucky, shortly after it arrived there from Adamstown in Lancaster County, Pennsylvania. With the quilt was a small slip of paper that read, "Friendship Quilt, dated 1856, made by women at Trindle Spring Church."

Hall immediately recognized the quilt's value. The fabrics are typical of those used in central Pennsylvania in the 1800s. The oak leaf and tulip appliqué pattern is a classic from that time period, and the hand piecing, appliqué, and quilting further supported the facts on the slip of paper. Even the feathered quilting pattern with cross-hatch and fan were clearly appropriate to that time period and geographic area. As a bonus, the quilt contained the signatures of the sixteen women who made it.

Trindle Spring Lutheran Church, constructed mid-1700s with later additions.

Trindle Spring
Lutheran Church, 1970s.

No quilt expert goes long without a visit to Lancaster, and at an annual quilt show there, Hall did some asking around and discovered that Mechanicsburg was only forty miles west. She made the trip to the Trindle Spring Church to see about bringing the quilt back to its roots.

It took the church nearly seven years to raise the funds to purchase this bit of their heritage, but it was brought back with a big celebration in 2010. The quilt now hangs in a specially designed case where it is protected from dirt and bright light. It is rotated regularly to reduce pressure on the fragile threads, and members of the church have located the graves of every woman who worked on that quilt. Connections have been made with descendants of the quilt makers, enabling them to reconnect with their roots now that the quilt is back where it started.

This quilt is a classic example of the quilts we documented. Some were made here; others were not. As a crossroads community, Cumberland County's quilts may have traveled more than others from the greater region. The Trindle Spring "friendship" quilt is the perfect introduction to those learning about the world of vintage quilts. It shows the ways in which quilts touch people and the value of researching and documenting these often forgotten heirlooms.

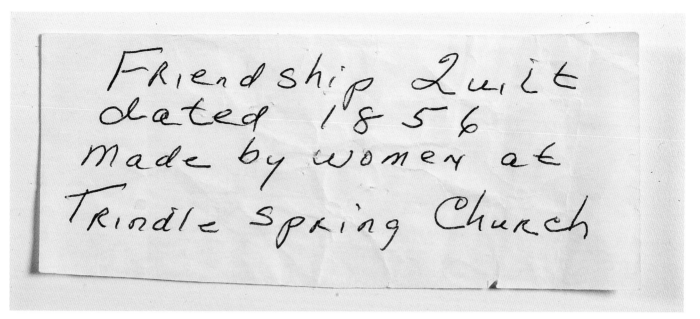

Paper label on the Oakleaf and Tulip friendship quilt when it was purchased in Kentucky. It was used to find Trindle Spring Lutheran Church in Mechanicsburg, where the quilt was made in 1856.

Gloria Leonard Hall with the friendship quilt.

Oakleaf and Tulip friendship quilt, 1856. The signature of each quilt maker appears in ink at center of the blocks: Barbara K. Schopf (Schopp), Mary (Schopf) Hertzler, Catherine (Strickler) Hertzler, Elizabeth (Coble) Sadler, Anna (Rupp) Coble, Mary (Erb) Hertzler, Mary (Bender) Hertzler, Susan (Snyder) Cocklin, Hannah (Gribble) Knisely, Fanny (Hurst/Horst) Eberly, Rebecca (Eberly) Hertzler, Eliza (Shuey) Eberly, Fannie (Beelman) Maust, Kate Eberly, Catherine (Frankenberger) Eberly, Mary A. (Spar) Brandt.

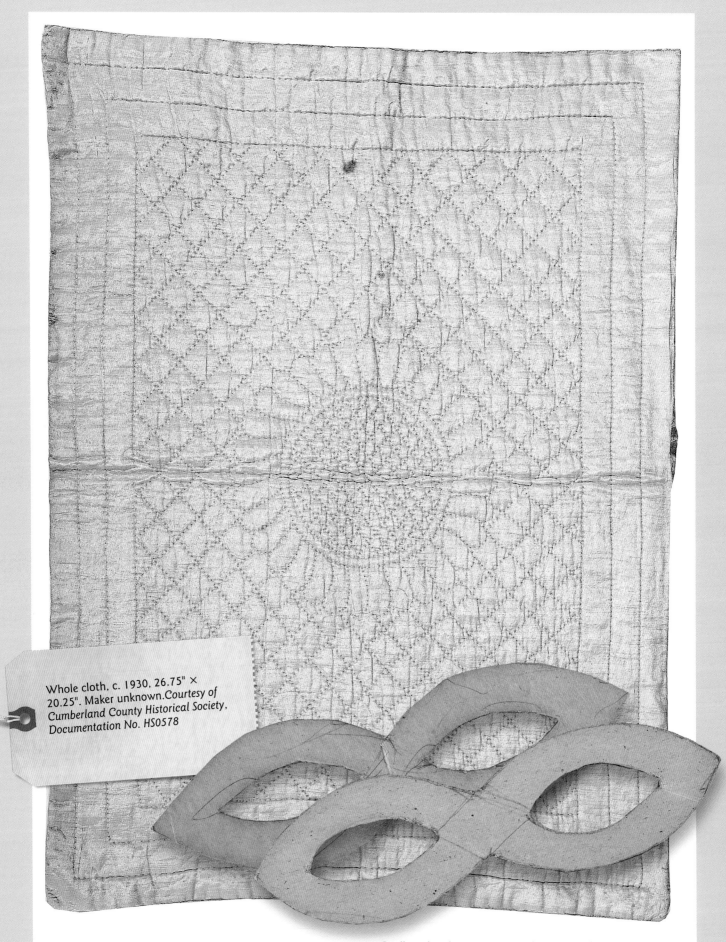

Whole cloth, c. 1930, 26.75" × 20.25". Maker unknown. Courtesy of Cumberland County Historical Society, Documentation No. HS0578

Cardboard quilting pattern used to trace a design on a quilt top before quilting. *Courtesy of Shirley Walker*

CHAPTER 2

Whole Cloth
and Simple Designs

The most basic quilt is made up of two layers of fabric with batting between them, and the three layers are held together with a quilting stitch. Quilted clothing, bedding, or wall hangings all start with this basic structure. Creativity comes in the quilting itself, the fabrics and their design, or some combination of the two. This chapter illustrates some of the simpler structures of quilts—either using whole cloth for both top and back, or very simple designs.

Quilted petticoat, begun in the 1800s, 38" × 43". Maker unknown. The waist is applied with woven tape that is used for ties; the petticoat has slits for pockets. *Courtesy of Margaret Schultz, Documentation No. BV0248*

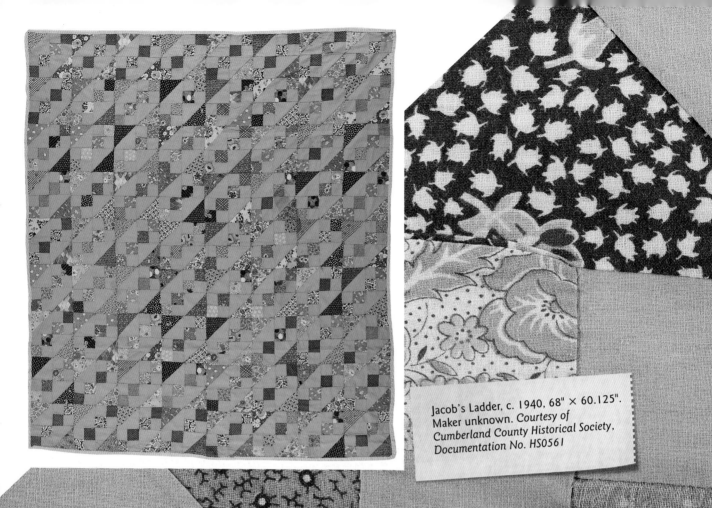

Jacob's Ladder, c. 1940, 68" × 60.125".
Maker unknown. Courtesy of
Cumberland County Historical Society,
Documentation No. HS0561

Strippy Quilt, c. 1840, 112" × 108.75".
Maker unknown. Courtesy of
Cumberland County Historical Society,
Documentation No. HS0580

Turkey Tracks, c. 1840, 10.5" × 10.5".
Maker unknown. Courtesy of Sandy
Harmon, Documentation No. BV0708

CUMBERLAND COUNTY, PA
QUILT DOCUMENTATION
BV 00708

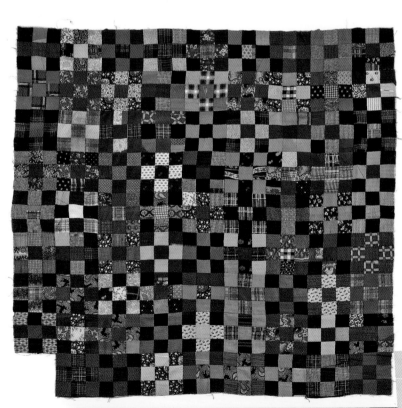

Nine-Patch, c. 1900, 71" × 70". Maker
unknown. Courtesy of John N.Reichert,
Documentation No. TM0633

25

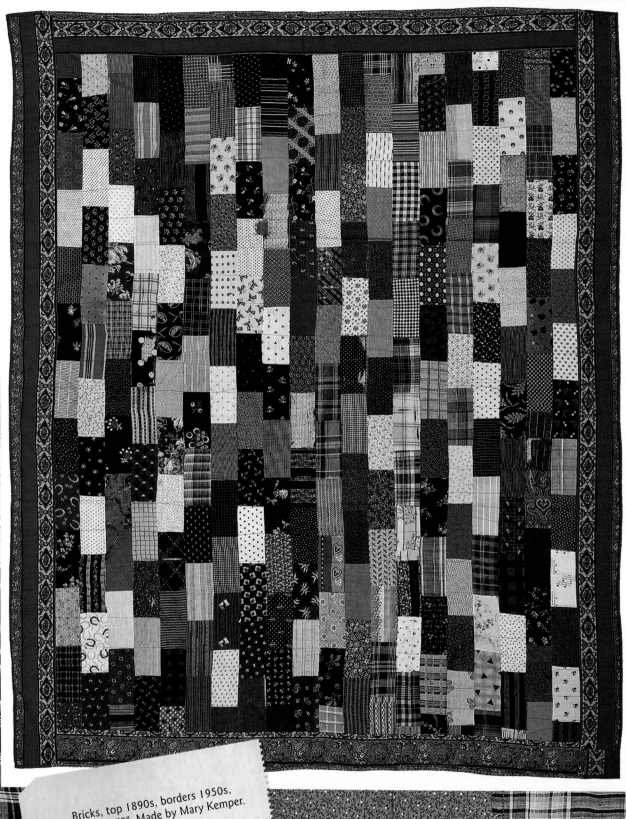

Bricks, top 1890s, borders 1950s, 87.5" × 73". Made by Mary Kemper. Courtesy of Martha Harry, Documentation No. TM0066

This patch quilt was made by my Great Grandmother Mary Martha Elizabeth Jacobs-Kemper. I received it about 1955. She made many dresses for me earlier. Some of the fabric dates back as early as 1888. If stored, the quilt needs to be rolled, not folded.

Martha Harry 2005

27

Nine-Patch, c. 1940, 97" × 77". Maker unknown, *Courtesy of Sandy Harmon, Documentation No. BV0671*

Trip Around the World, c. 1920, 88" × 83.5". Maker unknown. Courtesy of Deb Cooney, Documentation No. SM0065

Postage Stamp, c. 1930, 95" × 68". Made by sisters Romaine and Pauline Lebo. Courtesy of Shirley and Roy Lebo, Documentation No. TM0599

29

Sawtooth Strippy, c. 1850, 41" × 41".
Made by Mary Ann Gutshall Kutz.
Courtesy of Cumberland County Historical
Society, Documentation No. HS0587

Four-Patch, c. 1870, 67.5" ×32.5".
Maker unknown. Courtesy of John N.
Reichert, Documentation No. TM0634

Trip Around the World, c. 1890, 74" × 74". Made by Clara Farence. Courtesy of Rhoda Brough Funk, Documentation No. CU0649

Churn Dash, c. 1930, 78" ×64". Maker unknown. Courtesy of Betty Tritt, Documentation No. TM0090

Strips, Squares,
and Triangles

Most quilts are constructed from simple shapes pieced together—strips, squares, rectangles, and triangles. These basic forms yield a wide variety of patterns based on the arrangement of color and the contrast between light, medium, and dark colors. Some quilt patterns are classic and their names well known—Log Cabin, Flying Geese, and Nine-Patch are familiar to many. Other patterns are unique to a particular maker or look different based on color placement. The quilts in this chapter are examples of pieced quilts using primarily strips, squares, or triangles to create the design.

Jacob's Ladder, c. 1890, 78.5" × 67.5".
Maker unknown. Courtesy of Prudence
Sheely. Documentation No. TM0085

Broken Dishes, 1850, 75.5" × 71.5". Maker unknown. Courtesy of Cumberland County Historical Society, Documentation No. HS0449

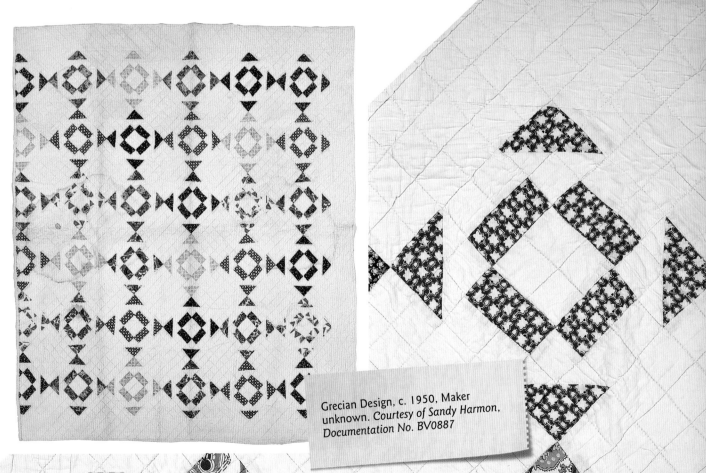

Grecian Design, c. 1950, Maker unknown. Courtesy of Sandy Harmon, Documentation No. BV0887

Delectable Mountains, c. 1920, 83.5" × 75". Made by sisters Romaine and Pauline Lebo. *Courtesy of Shirley and Roy Lebo, Documentation No. TM0597*

35

Ocean Waves, c. 1900, 41.5" × 30".
Maker unknown. Courtesy of Joseph
and Karen Buckley, Documentation
No. KB0007

Unnamed, c. 1860, 85.5" × 76.5".
Maker unknown. Courtesy of Debby
Cooney, Documentation No. SM0063

Pine Tree, c. 1940, 79.5" × 64". Maker unknown. Courtesy of Jean U. Tron, Documentation No. SM0046

Flying Geese, c. 1880, 81.5" × 80.5". Maker unknown. Courtesy of Sandy Harmon, Documentation No. BV0682

Tree of Life, 1896, 78.75" × 78".
Maker unknown. Courtesy of Carolyn
Winslow, Documentation No.
WH1035

Turkey Tracks/Flower Vase, 1915, 85" × 70.75". Maker unknown. Courtesy of Janet G. Wolgemuth, Documentation No. MV0291

Snail's Trail, c. 1910, 81" × 79". Maker unknown. *Courtesy of Sandy Harmon, Documentation No. BV0673*

Delectable Mountains, c. 1830, 98.75" × 95". Made by Linda Jacob. *Courtesy of Cumberland County Historical Society, Documentation No. HS0562*

Delectable Mountains (variation), 1841, 101.75" × 101.25". Made by Mary Jane Jamison. Courtesy of Cumberland County Historical Society, Documentation No. HS0565

Sawtooth Squares, c. 1900, 74" × 74". Maker unknown. Courtesy of Elizabeth Ann Burke, Documentation No. GR0161

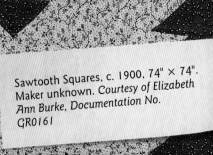

41

Log Cabin Barn Raising, c. 1860, 77.75" × 76.5". Made by Mary Jane Wingerd Gettel. Courtesy of Cumberland County Historical Society, Documentation No. HS0432

Log Cabin Barn Raising, c. 1880, 82" × 80.5". Made by Ellen Enck Williams. *Courtesy of Cumberland County Historical Society, Documentation No. HS0429*

String Quilt, c. 1940, 80" × 86". Maker unknown. *Courtesy of Betty A Mortlock, Documentation No. GR0539*

Log Cabin, 1879, 76.25" × 68.25". Made by Clara Ellen Anderson. Courtesy of Cumberland County Historical Society, Documentation No. HS0551

Spiderweb, c. 1930, 75" × 58.25". Made by Dora Melinda and Della Matilda Ewton. *Courtesy of Fay H. Shiflett, Documentation No. BV0323*

Windmill Blades, c. 1960, 78.25" × 79". Made by Jennie Schultz, Courtesy of Margaret Schultz, Documentation No. BV0273

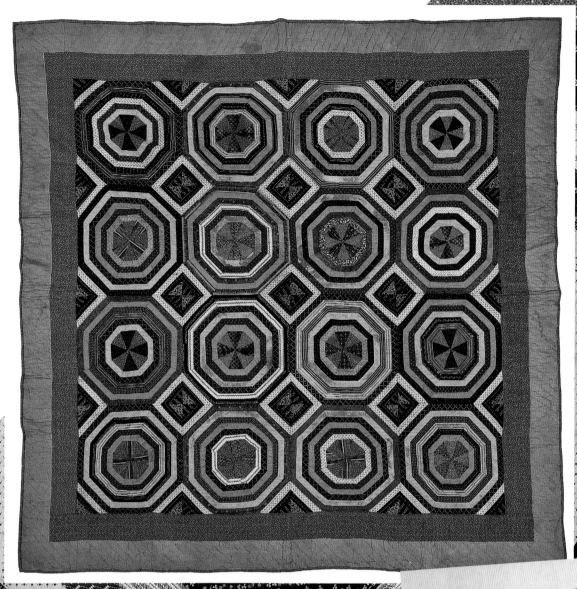

Cobweb, c. 1880, 89" × 90". Maker unknown. Courtesy of Margaret Shelly, Documentation No. BV0331

Lone Star, c. 1930, 70.25" × 70.25". Made by Mary Felmy. She made at least four Lone Stars in the 1930s. Anna and Tom Beckley own three, and Anna's niece, Kathryn Spangler Humbert of Danville, Pennsylvania, owns the fourth. *Courtesy of Tom and Anna Beckley, Documentation No. BV0191*

Stars

The quilts in this chapter use triangles, squares, or diamonds to make impressive stars or star-like patterns. The technical skills necessary to construct some of these quilts are considerable. Whether it involves the balance of color, perfect points, or the intricate layout of a large design such as the Lone Star, one can truly admire the workmanship of the women who made them.

Star of Bethlehem, c. 1840, 41" × 42".
Maker unknown. *Courtesy of John N. Reichert, Documentation No. TM0632*

Lone Star, c. 1930, 71.5" × 70".
Made by Mary Felmy. *Courtesy of Tom and Anna Beckley, Documentation No. BV0192*

Lone Star, c. 1930, 71.5" × 74".
Made by Mary Felmy. Courtesy of
Tom and Anna Beckley.
Documentation No. BV0193

Lone Star, c. 1890, 81" × 81". Maker
unknown. Courtesy of Joan Deibler,
Documentation No. GR0159

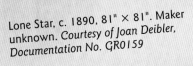

A. BINNER
1890

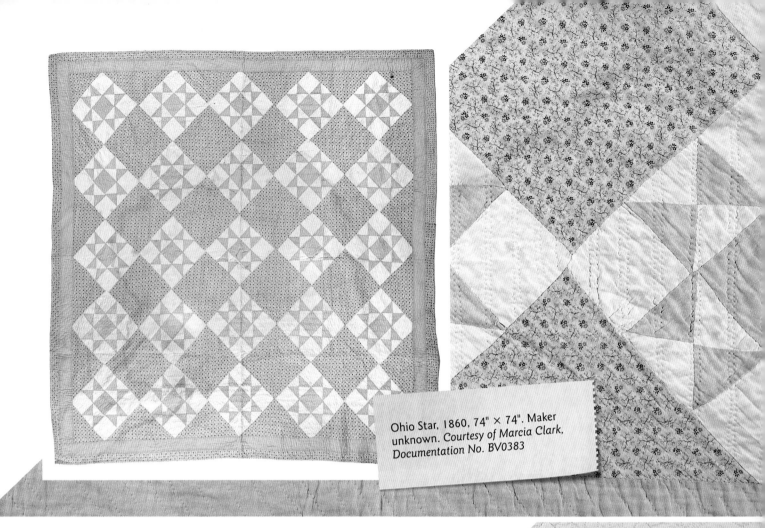

Ohio Star, 1860, 74" × 74". Maker unknown. *Courtesy of Marcia Clark, Documentation No. BV0383*

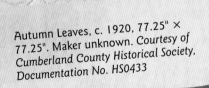

Autumn Leaves, c. 1920, 77.25" × 77.25". Maker unknown. *Courtesy of Cumberland County Historical Society, Documentation No. HS0433*

Ohio Star, c. 1900, 67" × 64.75". Made by Katie Miller Fogelsanger. Courtesy of Cumberland County Historical Society. Documentation No. HS0554

Carpenter's Wheel, c. 1870, 81.5" × 78.675". Maker unknown. Courtesy of Sandy Harmon, Documentation No. TM0768

Delectable Mountains, c. 1880, 89" × 89.5". Made by Ida Maria Wood. Courtesy of William Bamber, Documentation No. GR0532

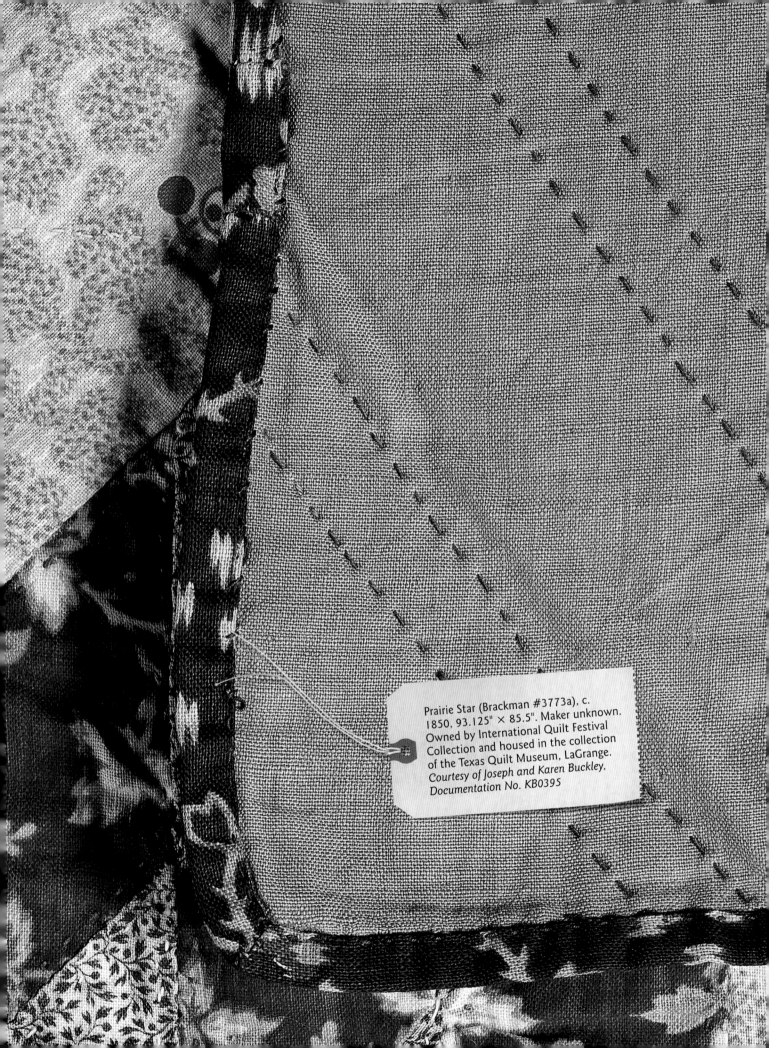

Prairie Star (Brackman #3773a), c.
1850, 93.125" × 85.5". Maker unknown.
Owned by International Quilt Festival
Collection and housed in the collection
of the Texas Quilt Museum, LaGrange.
Courtesy of Joseph and Karen Buckley,
Documentation No. KB0395

Feathered Star, c. 1840, 97" × 97".
Maker unknown. Courtesy of
Cumberland County Historical Society,
Documentation No. HS0567

Mariner's Compass, c. 1850, 74.75" × 74". Made by Mary Kutz. Courtesy of Cumberland County Historical Society, Documentation No. HS0552

Star of the East, 1941, 75" × 76.125".
Made by Adeline Merkel Detweiler.
Courtesy of Margaret Shelly,
Documentation No. BV0367

This quilt belongs
to

Richard P. Shelly,
made by his
Grandmother
Detweiler in the
Year of 1941.

Multiple Lone Star, c. 1840, 101" × 95.5". Made by Jane Matthews. Courtesy of Cumberland County Historical Society, Documentation No. HS0575

Feathered Star with center variation, c.
1870, 83.5" × 67.5". Maker unknown.
Courtesy of Joseph and Karen Buckley,
Documentation No. KB0010

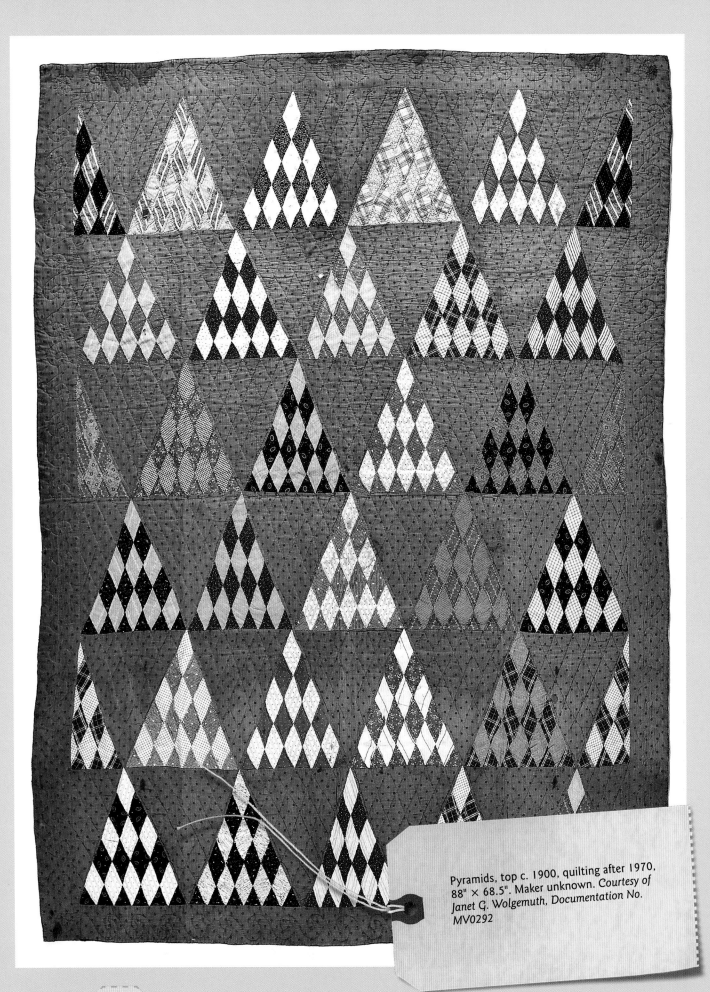

Pyramids, top c. 1900, quilting after 1970, 88" × 68.5". Maker unknown. Courtesy of Janet G. Wolgemuth, Documentation No. MV0292

Diamonds, Hexagons,
and Curves

The diamond shape creates interesting images based on color selection, balance of light, medium, and dark shades, and cutting the diamond into triangles. Curved pieces, as in the classic Dresden Plate pattern, add a sense of movement and grace. Hexagons lent an entirely new shape that proved popular with quilters and led to a wide variety of classic quilts.

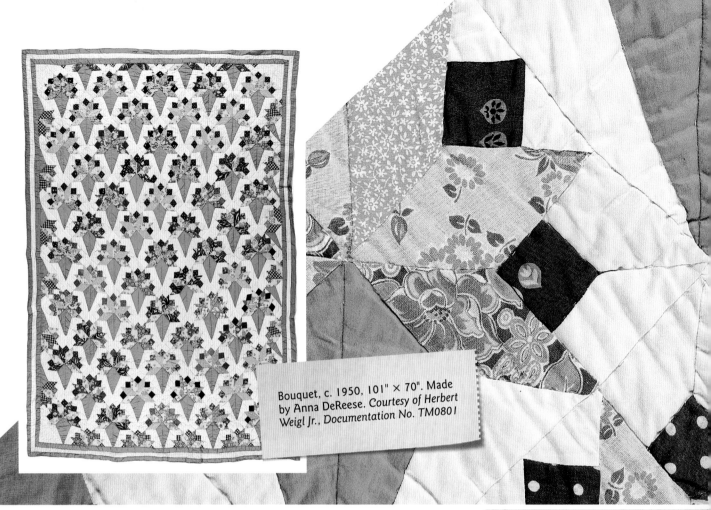

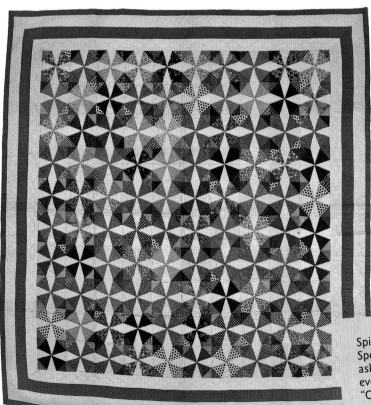

Bouquet, c. 1950, 101" × 70". Made by Anna DeReese. Courtesy of Herbert Weigl Jr., Documentation No. TM0801

Spiderweb, c. 1940, 93" × 93". Made by Jessie Spealman Deatrick. When the current owner asked his grandmother, the quiltmaker, if she ever participated in quilting bees, she replied, "Oh no, their stitches are not as small as mine." Courtesy of George and Phyllis Kegerreis, Documentation No. BV0260

Box quilt, c. 1940, 89" × 67.5". Made by Ann Catharine McDonald. Courtesy of Cletus A. Benjamin, Documentation No. GR0153

CUMBERLAND COUNTY, PA

box quilt made by ann Catharine McDonald for Cletus A. Benjamin — Made in 1940's

Dresden Plate, c. 1930, 106" ×
87.25". Maker unknown. Courtesy of
Carolyn Winslow, Documentation
No. WH1033

Cardboard pattern for
Dresden Plate. Courtesy
of Shirley Walker

ALICE MISHLER HOLL
1877-1951

Dresden Plate, c. 1930, 81.5" × 82".
Made by Alice Holl. Courtesy of Louise
Weldy, Documentation No. BV0243

71

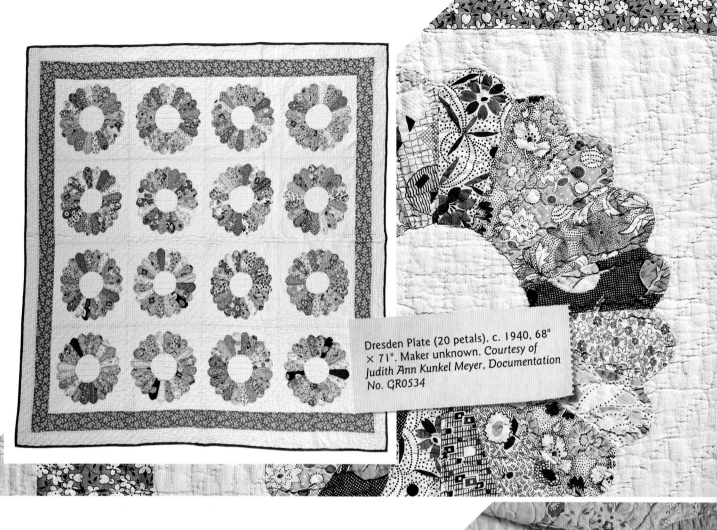

Dresden Plate (20 petals), c. 1940, 68" × 71". Maker unknown. Courtesy of Judith Ann Kunkel Meyer, Documentation No. GR0534

Dresden Plate, c. 1930, 87" × 79.5". Maker unknown. Courtesy of Dorene P. Benjamin, Documentation No. GR0155

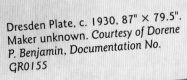

Dresden Plate, c. 1930, 92.5" × 74.5".
Maker unknown. Courtesy of R. Kathryn
Grabowski, Documentation No. TM0096

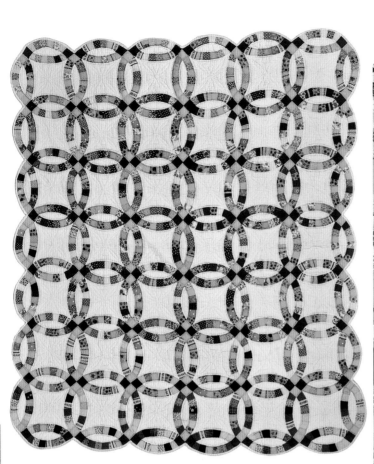

Double Wedding Ring, 1950, 81" × 68.5". Maker unknown. Courtesy of Evelyn Rebenstorff, Documentation No. MZ0470

Double Wedding Ring, 1974, 87.75" × 84". Maker unknown. Courtesy of Carolyn Winslow, Documentation No. WH1103

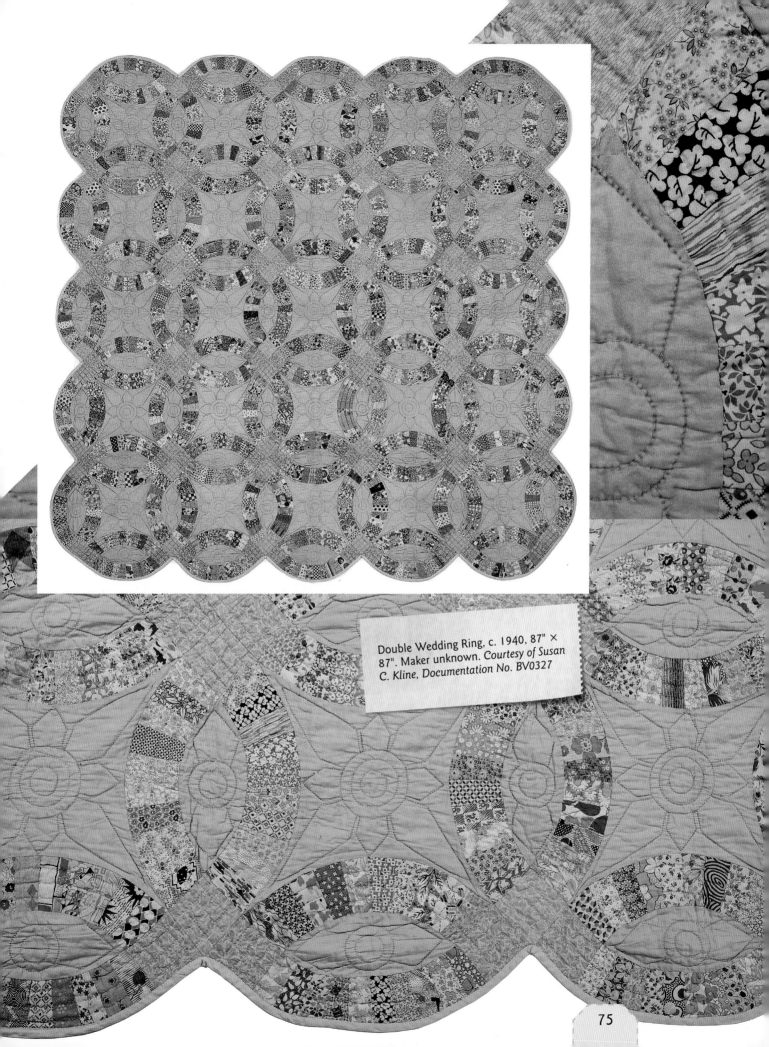

Double Wedding Ring, c. 1940, 87" × 87". Maker unknown. Courtesy of Susan C. Kline, Documentation No. BV0327

Hexagon variation, c. 1870, 81.5" × 73". Maker unknown. This is a typical Lancaster County quilt, identifiable by the colors and print backing. *Courtesy of Margaret Shelly, Documentation No. BV0343*

Hexagon variation, c. 1940, 86" × 73.75". Made by sisters Romaine and Pauline Lebo. *Courtesy of Shirley and Roy Lebo, Documentation No. TM0602*

Cardboard hexagon pattern for quilt blocks. *Courtesy of Shirley Walker*

Two-Sided Hexagon, c. 1940, 57.5" × 49.5". Maker unknown. *Courtesy of Jennifer Betar, Documentation No. TM0787*

Patchwork quilt made by Louise Uhl Kennedy in Johnstown, Cambria County, Pennsylvania, sometime in the late 1940s. Patches were left over from three Grandmother's Flower quilts she made for each of her three daughters. Material was probably purchased by her eldest daughter, Dorothy Kennedy Bollinger who had a good eye for color. Dorothy's mother-in-law and my grandmother's neighbor, Mrs. Sarah Martin, helped her with the quilting. She had a large back porch and the quilt frame was set up every summer for the ladies. Picture of my grandmother stitching on the quilt she made for my mother (Charlotte Kennedy Robson) is enclosed. My place was under the frame, using scraps of cloth for my dolls.

Judy Vetock
164 S. West St.
Carlisle, PA 17013
717-249-4067

Scrap Hexagons, c. 1950, 101" × 81". Made by Louise Kennedy. Courtesy of Judy Vetock, Documentation No. TM0626

79

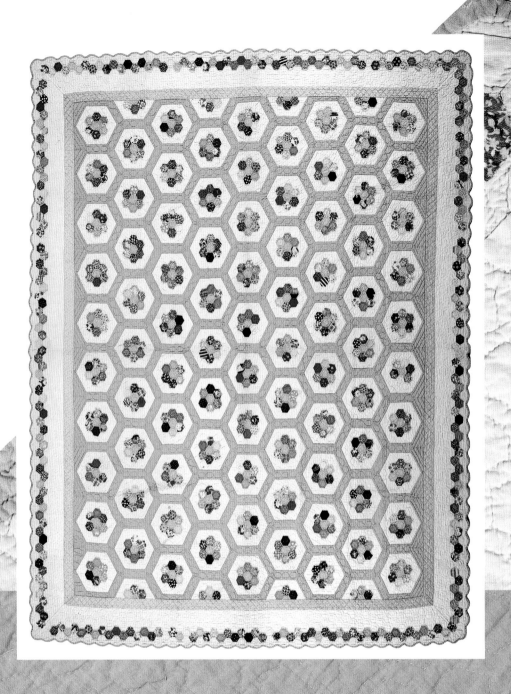

ELLEN CULP ROOSE
1863 — 1953

Dresden Plate, c. 1930, 88.25" × 73.5".
Made by Ellen Culp Roose. Courtesy of
Louise Weldy, Documentation No. BV0242

Grandmother's Flower Garden, c. 1930,
81.75" × 92". Made by Fredericka
Peppmiller. Courtesy of Janet Nelson,
Documentation No. SM0043

Appliqué

Appliqué is a technique for sewing fabric pieces onto a background. Whether the design is made from just one whole cloth, as in Hawaiian quilting, or from many small pieces, the appliqué quilt looks very different from those whose basic structure comes from pieced geometric shapes. Edges of the appliquéd pieces are often turned under and sewn down with very tiny stitches so that the separate pieces appear to be part of a whole design. The craftsmanship involved in producing these fine examples of appliqué is impressive.

Whig Rose, c. 1850, 43" × 43.25". Maker unknown. *Courtesy of Jim and Dawn Flower, Documentation No. TM0104*

Oak Leaf variation, c. 1850, 72" × 73.25". Maker unknown. Courtesy of John N. Reichert, Documentation No. TM0637

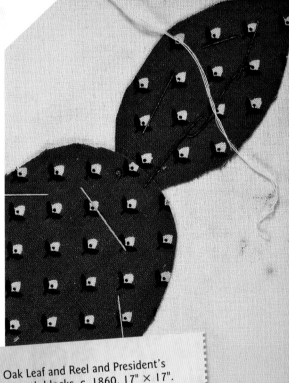

Oak Leaf and Reel and President's Wreath blocks, c. 1860, 17" × 17". Maker unknown. Courtesy of John N. Reichert, Documentation No. TM0636

Oak Leaf and Reel variation, c. 1850, 96" × 95.6". Made by Mary Landis. Courtesy of Cumberland County Historical Society, Documentation No. HS0589

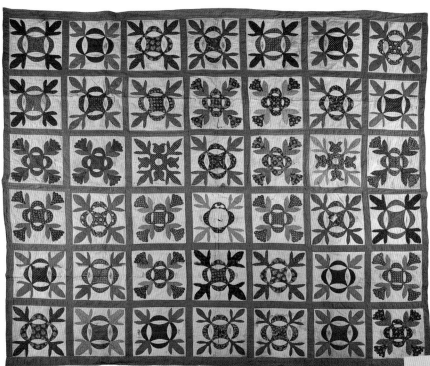

Red and green appliqué, c. 1850, 102.375" × 89.5". Maker unknown. Courtesy of Virginia Dougherty Goodyear, Documentation No. TM0101

Nine Block Appliqué with Oak Leaves, c. 1840, 93.75" × 90.5". Made by Margaret Miller. Courtesy of Cumberland County Historical Society, Documentation No. HS0579

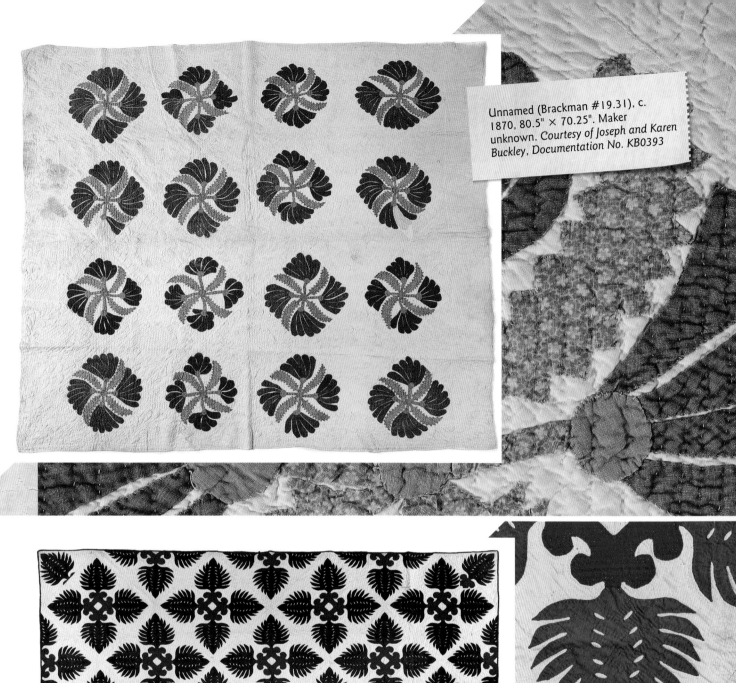

Floral Appliqué variation, c. 1870, 71" × 70.25". Maker unknown. Courtesy of Joseph and Karen Buckley, Documentation No. KB0009

Whig Rose, c. 1850, 87.625" × 87.375". Maker unknown. Courtesy of Joseph and Karen Buckley, Documentation No. KB0011

Appliqued Medallion, c. 1860, 84" × 84". Maker unknown. Owned by International Quilt Festival Collection and housed in the collection of the Texas Quilt Museum, LaGrange. Courtesy of Joseph and Karen Buckley, Documentation No. KB0406

Prince's Feather or Princess Feather, c. 1860, 88" × 86". Made by Jessie Deatrick. Courtesy of George and Phyllis Kegerreis, Documentation No. BV0261

Prince's Feather or Princess Feather, c. 1930, 88.5" × 88.5". Made by Jessie Deatrick. Courtesy of George and Phyllis Kegerreis, Documentation No. BV0262

Prince's Feather or Princess Feather, c. 1860, 91.5" × 90". Maker unknown. Courtesy of Cumberland County Historical Society, Documentation No. HS0444

Red and green floral appliqué, c. 1880, 81" × 73". Maker unknown. Courtesy of Cumberland County Historical Society, Documentation No. HS0572

92

Four Tulips (Loretta's Rose), c. 1890, 101" × 85.5". Maker unknown. Courtesy of John N. Reichert, Documentation No. TM0638

Hawaiian Appliqué, c. 1930, 89" × 94". Maker unknown. Owned by International Quilt Festival Collection and housed in the collection of the Texas Quilt Museum, LaGrange. Courtesy of Joseph and Karen Buckley, Documentation No. KB0399

Rose Wreath Applique with Four Elements, c. 1860, 90.5" × 90.25". Made by Mary "Polly" Bixler. Courtesy of Linda Stoltz, Documentation No. GR0517

Album Quilt, c. 1880, 94" × 94".
Maker unknown. Courtesy of
Cumberland County Historical
Society. Documentation No. HS0573

Three Tulips in a Pot, c. 1940,
71" × 75". Maker unknown.
Courtesy of Sandy Harmon,
Documentation No. BV0874

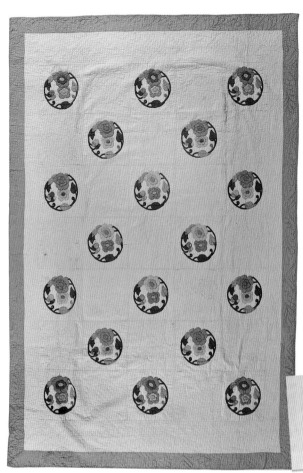

Floral Appliqué, c. 1930, 94" × 64.5". Made by Mary Dibble Bracket. Courtesy of Cumberland County Historical Society, Documentation No. HS0581

Pansies, c. 1950, 85" × 71.5". Maker unknown. Courtesy of Evelyn Rebenstorff, Documentation No. MZ0504

Pennsylvania Album, c. 1850, 82.375" × 81.5". Maker unknown. Owned by International Quilt Festival Collection and housed in the collection of the Texas Quilt Museum, LaGrange. *Courtesy of Joseph and Karen Buckley, Documentation No. KB0014*

Flowers and Bubbles, c. 1930, 78" × 78". Made by Annie McCracken Spealman. When Annie married A. Franklin Spealman, her family disowned her. After moving with him to York Springs, Pennsylvania, she never heard from her family again. The current owners got the information about Annie's parents from a note labeled, "To be used only in an emergency." *Courtesy of George and Phyllis Kegerreis, Documentation No. BV0253*

D.D.K
GrAnd
MOTHer.
1933.

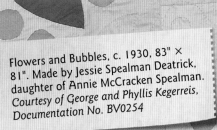

Flowers and Bubbles, c. 1930, 83" × 81". Made by Jessie Spealman Deatrick, daughter of Annie McCracken Spealman. Courtesy of George and Phyllis Kegerreis, Documentation No. BV0254

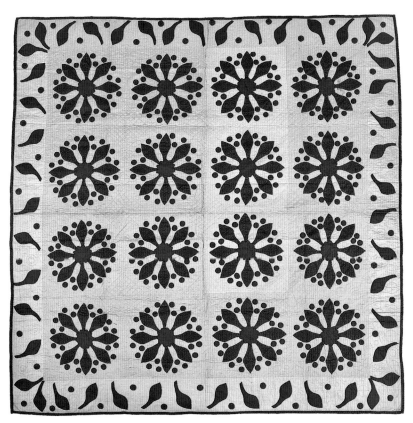

Flowers and Bubbles, c. 1930, 83.5" × 83.5". Made by Jessie Spealman Deatrick. Courtesy of George and Phyllis Kegerreis, Documentation No. BV0259

Sweet Pea (Mountain Mist pattern), c. 1940, 80.25" × 96". Maker unknown. *Courtesy of Patricia Gildner, Documentation No. TM0606*

Flower Appliqué, 1875, 85" × 85.5". Maker unknown. *Courtesy of Carolyn Winslow, Documentation No. WH1038*

Mountain Mist Poinsettia, c. 1930, 95" × 77". Made by sisters Romaine and Pauline Lebo. Courtesy of Shirley and Roy Lebo, Documentation No. TM0601

Yo-Yo Flowers, c. 1930, 80.5" × 70.5". Maker unknown. Courtesy of Sandy Harmon, Documentation No. BV0658

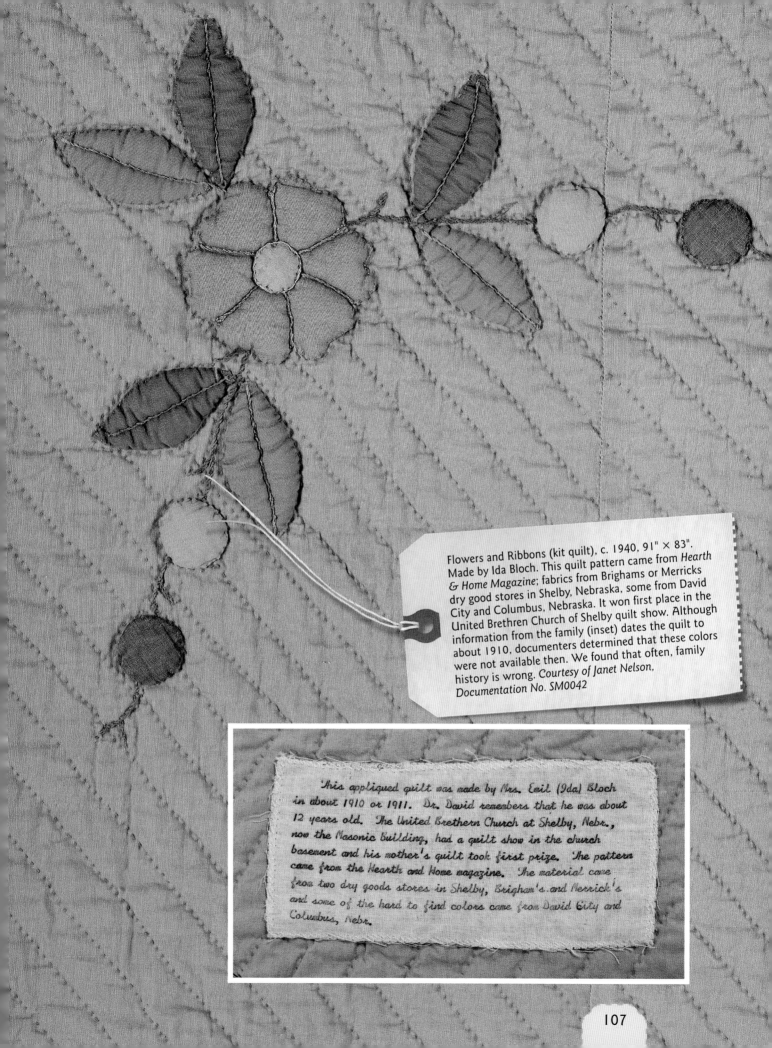

Flowers and Ribbons (kit quilt), c. 1940, 91" × 83". Made by Ida Bloch. This quilt pattern came from *Hearth & Home Magazine*; fabrics from Brighams or Merricks dry good stores in Shelby, Nebraska, some from David City and Columbus, Nebraska. It won first place in the United Brethren Church of Shelby quilt show. Although information from the family (inset) dates the quilt to about 1910, documenters determined that these colors were not available then. We found that often, family history is wrong. *Courtesy of Janet Nelson, Documentation No. SM0042*

This appliqued quilt was made by Mrs. Emil (Ida) Bloch in about 1910 or 1911. Dr. David remembers that he was about 12 years old. The United Brethren Church at Shelby, Nebr., now the Masonic Building, had a quilt show in the church basement and his mother's quilt took first prize. The pattern came from the Hearth and Home magazine. The material came from two dry goods stores in Shelby, Brigham's and Merrick's and some of the hard to find colors came from David City and Columbus, Nebr.

Feathered Star Enhanced, c. 1900, 75" × 75".
Made by Mary Elizabeth Webber or Mrs.
David Landis. Courtesy of Cumberland County
Historical Society, Documentation No. HS0440

Mixed

and Variety

Some quilts don't fit into one category. Quilters often use a mixture of techniques to create their design. Others, like the Cathedral Windows and Yo-Yo patterns, are simply constructed differently from other quilts. The Yo-Yo is made of many small circles sewn together and may not be technically considered a quilt, given that there are no multiple sandwiched layers, but it is generally considered a form of quilting. The Cathedral Window gets quilted as it is constructed, so it doesn't contain batting. These are interesting variations on our quilting tradition.

Pomegranates, c. 1880, 85.25" × 70.5". Maker unknown. Courtesy of Margaret (Peg) Hassinger, Documentation No. BV0777

Basket, 1890, 87.25" × 76.25". Made by Mary Heminway. Courtesy of Cumberland County Historical Society, Documentation No. HS0430

Framed Turkey Tracks, 1866, 87.5" × 72". Maker unknown. Courtesy of Cumberland County Historical Society, Documentation No. HS0431

Hummingbird (Brackman #445.9), c. 1930, 96.75" × 74.5". Maker unknown. Courtesy of Susan C. Kline. Documentation No. BV0328

Lily, c. 1850, 85" × 81". Maker unknown. Courtesy of Joseph and Karen Buckley, Documentation No. KB0414

Cathedral Window, 1973. 73.25" × 79.75". Maker unknown. Courtesy of Sandy Harmon. Documentation No. BV0875

Carolina Lily, c. 1850, 83" × 81.5". Maker unknown. Courtesy of Cumberland County Historical Society, Documentation No. HS0564

Bethlehem Star, 1850, 38" × 37.5".
Maker unknown. Courtesy of John N.
Reichert, Documentation No. TM0631

Appliqué Medallion with Courthouse Steps border, c. 1890, 82" × 76.5". Maker unknown. It seems that the medallion portion may have been done earlier than the pieced borders. The medallion dates to circa 1860 and the finished quilt to circa 1890. In the medallion there are triangles and squares of cheater cloth. *Courtesy of Virginia Dougherty Goodyear, Documentation No. TM0099*

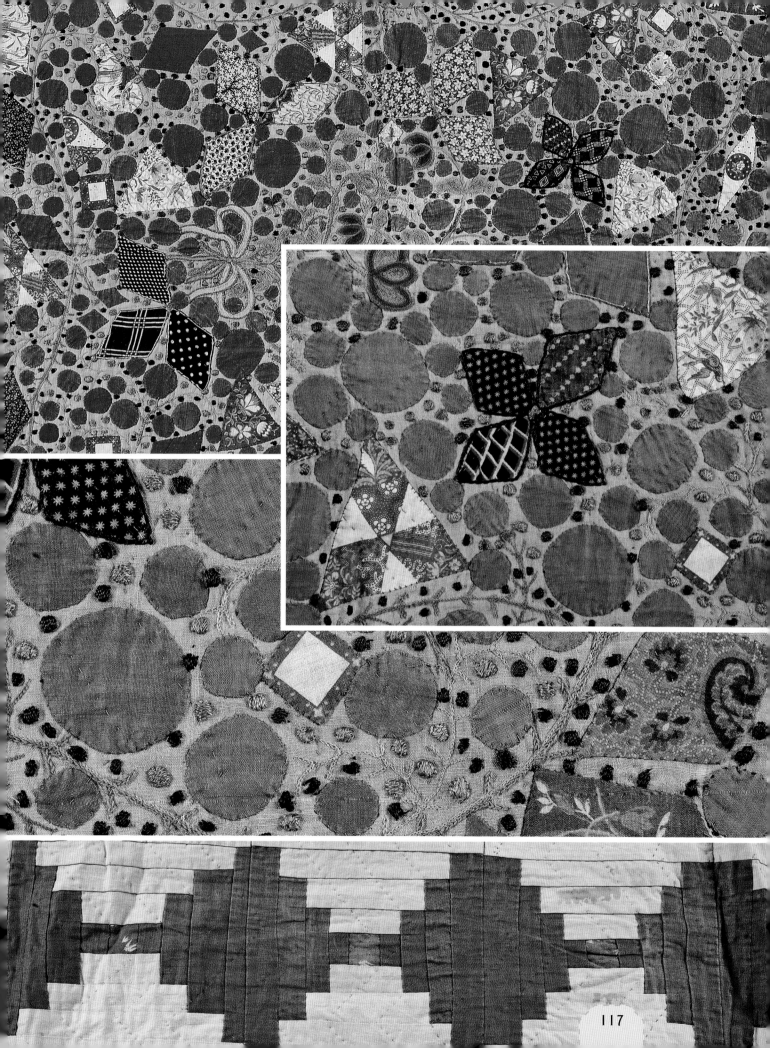

Yo-Yo Blocks with Yo Yo Fringe, c. 1920, 79" × 60". Made by Lillie Almeda Kutz Bender. Lillie Bender's husband William, a ticket agent for the Cumberland Valley Railroad in Newville and Carlisle, bought bags of scraps for twenty-five cents from the Carlisle Garment Co. (the maker of the Molly Pitcher dresses) on 44 North Bedford Street in Carlisle. She made up her own quilting designs based on the scraps she had to work with. Lillie would have made this quilt for a daughter, indicated by the green trim (sons' quilts were trimmed in blue), upon her marriage. *Courtesy of Lillie Ann Foster, Documentation No. GR0528*

Lillie (Kutz) Bender

Yo-Yo, c. 1930, 92" × 82". Maker
unknown. Courtesy of Cumberland
County Historical Society,
Documentation No. HS0569

Ocean Waves with redwork centers, 1891,
75" × 74". Maker unknown. The initials
(opposite page) may denote the owner, a
contributor, or dedication to someone.
*Courtesy of Sandy Harmon, Documentation
No. BV0680*

CHAPTER 8

Embroidered Quilts
and Sunbonnets

Embroidery is yet another quilting technique. The popular Penny Square and Redwork patterns were often embroidered and later set into a quilt. Sometimes additional pieced blocks were used to accentuate the setting of the embroidered blocks. Other embroidery patterns came from kits or were designed by their makers.

Another popular group of quilts, which we are referring to as Sunbonnets, combines appliqué and embroidery. Many of these designs depict a stylized figure with the face hidden by a hat or bonnet.

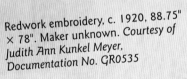

Redwork embroidery, c. 1920, 88.75" × 78". Maker unknown. Courtesy of Judith Ann Kunkel Meyer, Documentation No. GR0535

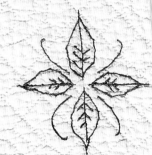

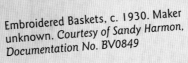

Penny Quilt, 1910, 73" × 58.5". Made by Edna Merkel. The quilt name is derived from the fact that the squares were purchased for one cent. Courtesy of Margaret Shelly, Documentation No. BV0365

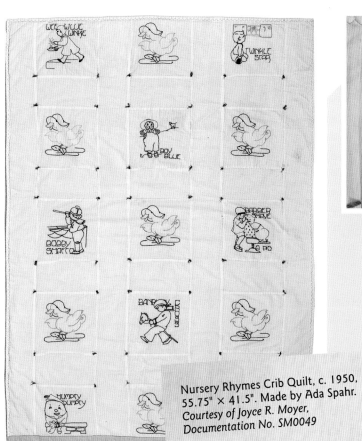

Nursery Rhymes Crib Quilt, c. 1950, 55.75" × 41.5". Made by Ada Spahr. Courtesy of Joyce R. Moyer, Documentation No. SM0049

Redwork Embroidery, 1915, 76.5" × 68". Made by Mary Leow, Courtesy of Sally John, Documentation No. NK0203

Bible quilt, c. 1930, 85.5" × 68.75". Made by Caroline Austin. Courtesy of Margaret Shelly, Documentation No. BV0346

Cottage and Flowers, 1931, 90" ×
71.5". Made by Mildred Keeseman.
Courtesy of Nancy Davey,
Documentation No. TM0114

MADE BY MILDRED MAE SHUMAN.
FEBRUARY 18, 1931.

Bucilla Double Bedspread and Bolster
#1251 Embroidered Floral, c. 1930,
78.5" × 64.25". Maker unknown.
Courtesy of Sandy Harmon,
Documentation No. TM0763

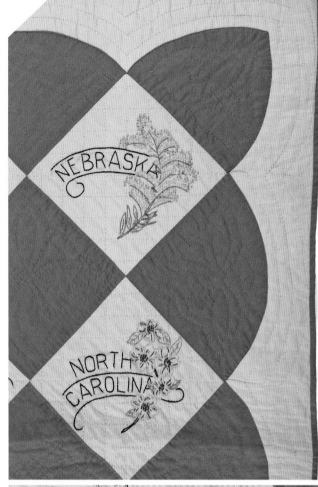

Embroidered State Flower blocks, c. 1950, 75" × 99". Made by mother-and-daughter team Anne Verle Miller and Mary Stoner. Anne pieced the quilt and Mary hand-quilted it. Courtesy of Claudia Lehman, Documentation No. TM0806

Mother Goose Quilt, 1945, 45" × 33.5". Made by Cora Frank. *Courtesy of Jane Landis, Documentation No. TM0812*

Embroidered quilt, c. 1930, 69.5" × 63". Maker unknown. *Courtesy of Betty Tritt, Documentation No. TM0092*

Sunbonnet Sue, c. 1930. Maker unknown. Courtesy of Sandy Harmon, Documentation No. BV0848

Southern Belle, c. 1950, 84" × 75". Made by Martha Garrett. The quilt is made of fabrics left over from making dresses and tops. *Courtesy of Adele Rall, Documentation No. BV0653*

Parasol Ladies, c. 1950, 79.5" × 69". Made by Sarah Reed. *Courtesy of Donna Lohman, Documentation No. MZ0488*

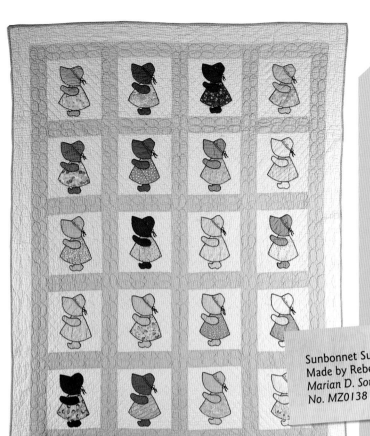

Sunbonnet Sue, c. 1930, 93" × 70.5".
Made by Rebecca Dunn. Courtesy of
Marian D. Soutner, Documentation
No. MZ0138

Sunbonnet Sue and Overall Bill, 1950, 38"
× 41". Made by Blanche Viola Campbell
Sheasley. Courtesy of Dr. Ann Smith
Greimer, Documentation No. BV0240

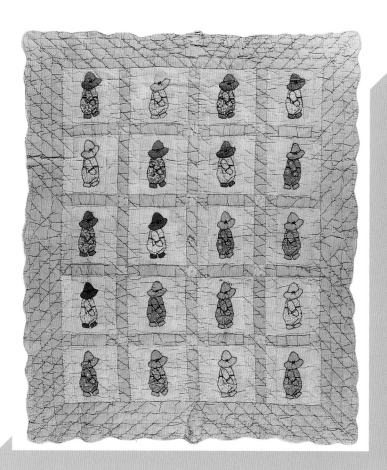

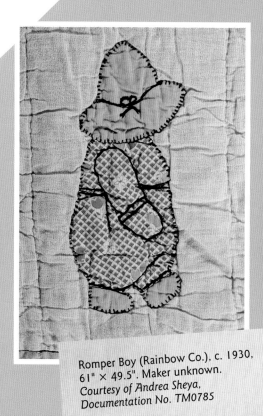

Romper Boy (Rainbow Co.), c. 1930, 61" × 49.5". Maker unknown. Courtesy of Andrea Sheya, Documentation No. TM0785

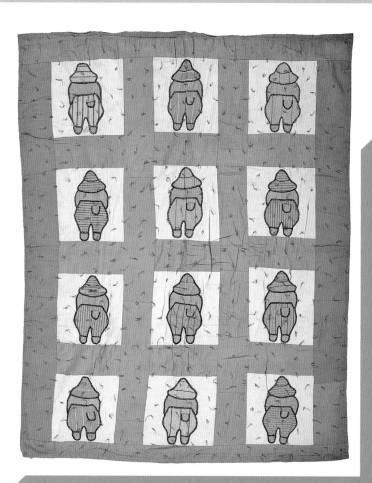

Overall Sam, c. 1930, 53" × 67". Made by Teresa A. Wolf Kegerreis. Courtesy of George and Phyllis Kegerreis, Documentation No. BV049

Chester Smee

rlig

Mrs

MILDRED COKE
IN MEMORY OF GRANDMOTHER

very

Lou

David D. McCoy

ell

Virg

IN MEMORY OF
MAXWELL GRAHAM

Friendship/signature fundraiser quilt, 1932, 71"
× 66". Made by Newville Methodist Church
women in an annual quilting bee for auction.
People paid ten cents to have their name on the
quilt. Reverend Darrell F. Stone purchased the
quilt for $25, using an entire month's pay.
*Courtesy of Charles Lehner Stone, Documentation
No. BV0244*

er

ree

ictor C. Smee

CHAPTER 9

Signature Quilts
and Special Events

There is a long tradition of quilts with signatures as a major focus. Signature quilts might have been made as a fundraiser, with individuals purchasing a block with their name on it. Names could be embroidered, stamped, or written in ink. Other signature quilts were made as gifts, with various individuals contributing a signed block, and then the blocks would be sewn into a quilt and given as a gift.

There are other ways to make a unique quilt for a specific event or commemoration. Often there are clues in the quilt design or in labels, signatures, or other documentation to indicate its function.

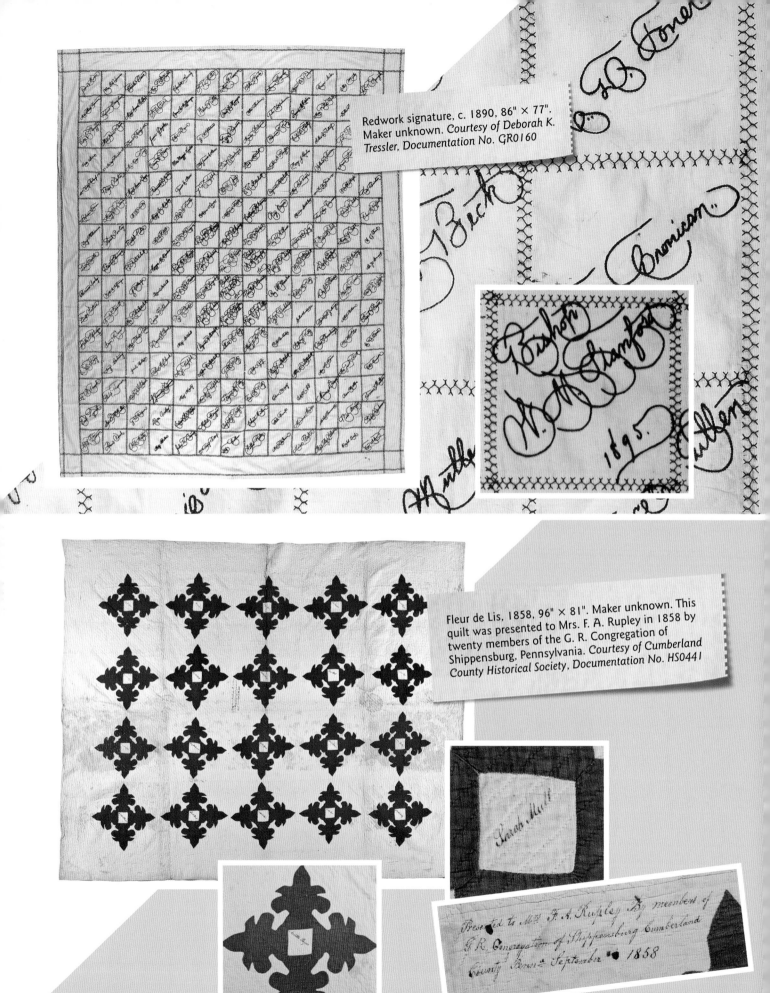

Redwork signature, c. 1890, 86" × 77".
Maker unknown. *Courtesy of Deborah K.
Tressler, Documentation No. GR0160*

Fleur de Lis, 1858, 96" × 81". Maker unknown. This
quilt was presented to Mrs. F. A. Rupley in 1858 by
twenty members of the G. R. Congregation of
Shippensburg, Pennsylvania. *Courtesy of Cumberland
County Historical Society, Documentation No. HS0441*

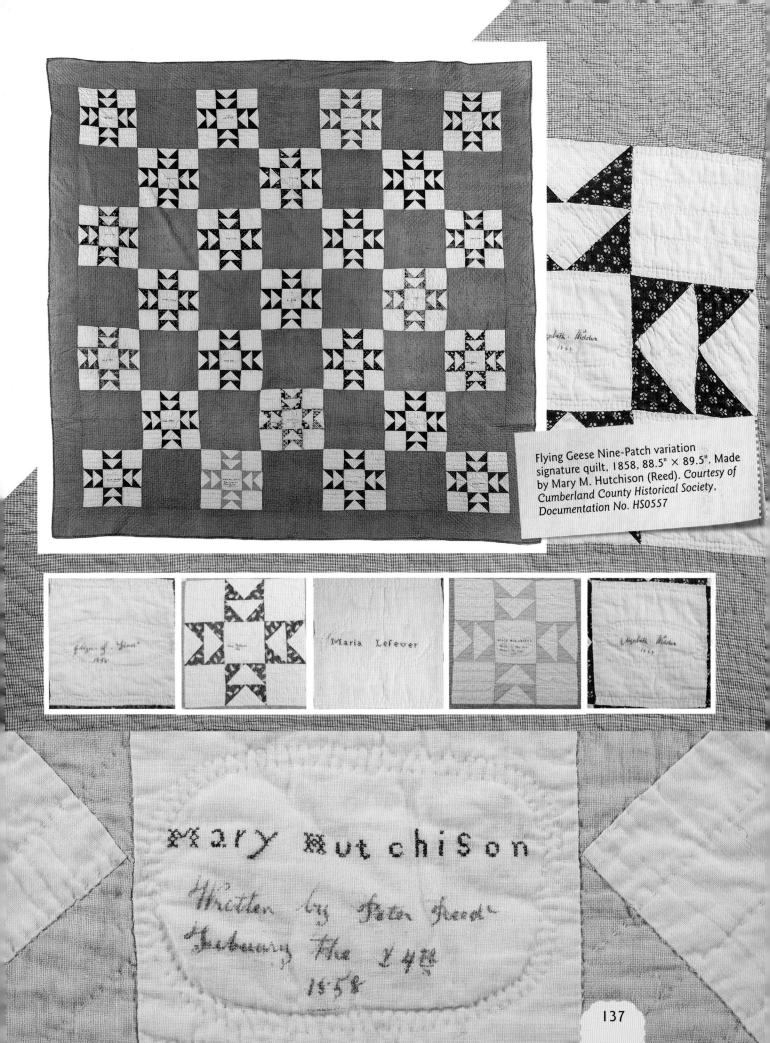

Flying Geese Nine-Patch variation signature quilt, 1858, 88.5" × 89.5". Made by Mary M. Hutchison (Reed). *Courtesy of Cumberland County Historical Society, Documentation No. HS0557*

Variable Star signature quilt, 1898, 85.5" × 77.5". Attributed to Agnes Myers. It is not known if the children's names on this quilt are children who lived in the area served by the Dickinson Post Office or if they are the quilt maker's students, but ten of the names were students at Dickinson Centerville School in January 1902. *Courtesy of Cumberland County Historical Society, Documentation No. HS0434*

Wheel, 1881–1887, 90.5" × 86.25". Maker unknown. Owned by International Quilt Festival Collection and housed in the collection of the Texas Quilt Museum, LaGrange. Courtesy of Joseph and Karen Buckley, Documentation No. KB0013

Rolling Stone, 1848, 88" × 89". Maker unknown. Courtesy of Joseph and Karen Buckley, Documentation No. KB0412

139

This Signature Quilt was made by
members of Immaculate Conception Church
in Dudley, PA. Finished April 1, 1907
Won by KATHRYN REILY LEWIS
given to MARGUERITE BRANNIGAN
and passed to her nephew
EDWARD R. LEWIS in 1975

Dresden Plate, 1907, 78" × 76.5". Made by women of Immaculate Conception Catholic Church. This signature quilt was made to raise money for the Immaculate Conception Church in Dudley, Huntington County, Pennsylvania. People paid ten cents to have their name put on the quilt. It was then raffled to raise more funds. Catherine Reilly Lewis won the quilt with signatures of Theodore Roosevelt, United Mineworkers president John Mitchell, Pennsylvania governor Samuel Pennypacker, Andrew Carnegie, and others. *Courtesy of Lois K. Lewis, Documentation No. MZ0137*

Signature Album quilt, c. 1930, 88.5" × 67". Maker unknown. Four generations of the current owner's family are represented on this quilt. Many names are friends and neighbors. It is believed to have been made as a wedding gift. *Courtesy of R. Kathryn Grabowski, Documentation No. TM0094*

Signature sampler, 1898, 69.5" × 81.5". Made by school families for Barbara Dohner Berger, a teacher at School District No. 8 in Miami County, Ohio, when she resigned from teaching to get married. *Courtesy of Sara B. Lenhert, Documentation No. MV0306*

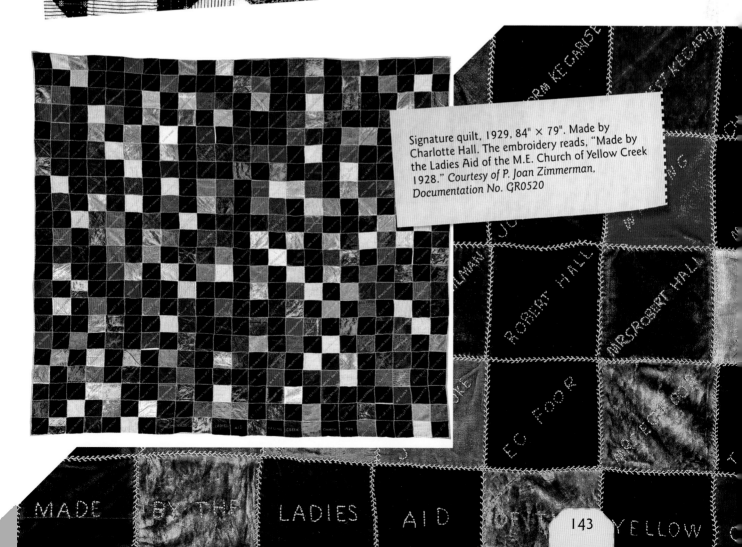

Signature quilt, 1929, 84" × 79". Made by Charlotte Hall. The embroidery reads, "Made by the Ladies Aid of the M.E. Church of Yellow Creek 1928." *Courtesy of P. Joan Zimmerman, Documentation No. GR0520*

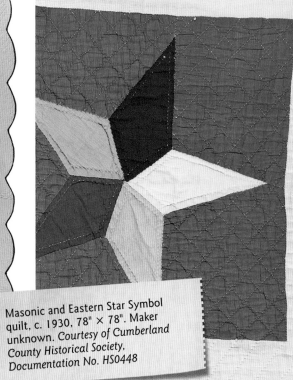

Masonic and Eastern Star Symbol quilt, c. 1930, 78" × 78". Maker unknown. Courtesy of Cumberland County Historical Society, Documentation No. HS0448

Tobacco Felts, c. 1930, 69.5" × 65". Made by Lillie Paxton. Courtesy of Judy Barbour, Documentation No. TM0089

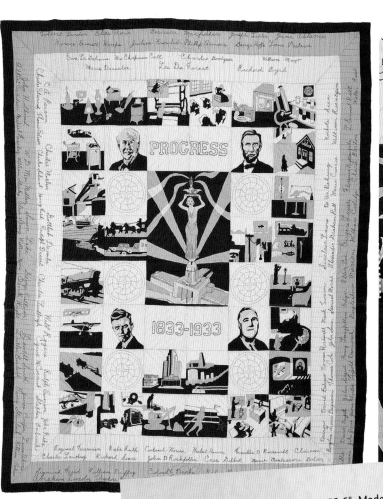

Century of Progress, 1933, 96.5" × 75.5". Made by Clarence and Linda Rebenstorff. This quilt was made for the 1933 Century of Progress World's Fair in Chicago. It represents inventions and progress from 1833 to 1933 in aviation, farm machinery, education, and art, among others. The names around the outside are outstanding contributors in their respective fields. The modern woman in the center represents giving women "credit for helping man achieve his dreams." *Courtesy of Evelyn Rebenstorff, Documentation No. MZ0475*

1833-1933

Crazy Quilts

The Crazy Quilt became popular in the late 1800s and remains a popular design today. Scraps of fabric, arranged in a seemingly haphazard manner, provide the backdrop for showing off fancy embroidery and embellishments. Many Crazy Quilts were made of scraps of silk, velvet, and other fancy fabrics with lavishly detailed handwork. Although some of those fabrics have deteriorated badly, many exquisite examples of this style can be found, along with more modest versions.

Crazy Quilt, 1889, 70" × 58.25". Made by Mary Hunter. The quilt maker was the wife of John Hunter of Hunter Fan and Hunter Arms companies; he also was a farmer and helped build the Erie Canal. *Courtesy of Tom Ward, Documentation No. GR0150*

Flower Appliqué, c. 1900, 69" × 66". Maker unknown. Courtesy of Cumberland County Historical Society, Documentation No. HS0424

Crazy Quilt, 1931, 18" × 18". Made by sisters Romaine and Pauline Lebo. Courtesy of Shirley and Roy Lebo, Documentation No. TM0596

Crazy Quilt, 1885, 57" × 56.5".
Made by Minnie Hodgman. Courtesy
of Kathryn R. Kellie, Documentation
No. NK0205

Crazy Quilt, 1883, 73.5" × 73.125".
Maker unknown. Courtesy of
Cumberland County Historical Society,
Documentation No. HS0447

Annie.

J. G. K.

J. K.

E. W. K.

Crazy quilt, c. 1890, 79.5" × 79".
Made by Jane Martin. Courtesy of
Cumberland County Historical Society,
Documentation No. HS0553

154

Crazy Quilt, 1882, 68.25" × 68".
Made by Mary Emminger. Courtesy of
Cumberland County Historical
Society, Documentation No. HS0574

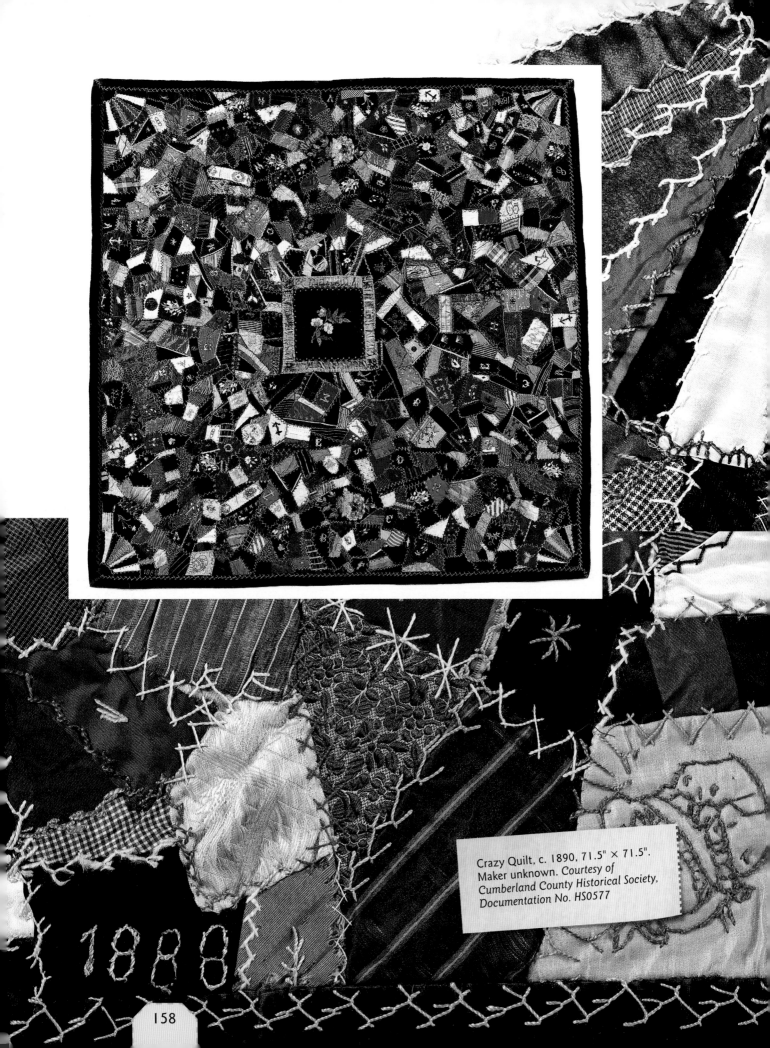

Crazy Quilt, c. 1890, 71.5" × 71.5".
Maker unknown. Courtesy of
Cumberland County Historical Society,
Documentation No. HS0577

1888

TO MY SISTER

THERE IS A SOFT AND
GENTLE FORM,
WHICH OFT BEFORE MY
MEMORY SPRINGS;
RECALLING CHILDHOODS
WITH HAPPY HOURS,
WITH ALL THEIR BRIGHT
IMAGININGS;

THAT STILL TO ME A
GUARDIAN SAINT,
CALL'S BACK THE THOUGHT
THAT'S PRONE TO ERR,
FORBIDING OUGHT THAT E'ER
COULD CAUSE,
A SISTERS BLUSH, A
SISTERS TEAR.

1885

1886

1887

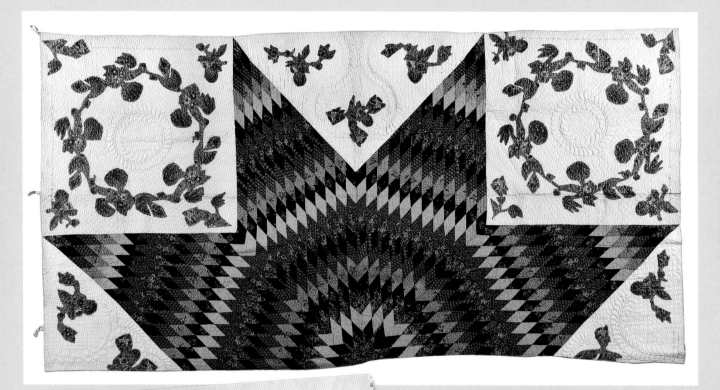

One-half Lone Star, c. 1850, 104" × 54". Maker unknown. This exquisite Lone Star with appliqué has been cut right down the center. The same thing has occurred with other quilts to split a quilt between family members, though the reason for cutting this one is unknown, as is the whereabouts of the other half. Despite the damage, it remains an interesting historical quilt, though we do not recommend this as the best way to pass down a vintage quilt. *Courtesy of Cumberland County Historical Society, Documentation No. HS0576*

Finding and Caring
for Vintage Quilts

Many vintage quilts are stored in museums where they are periodically put on display. Those quilts are never washed, mended, or touched by dirty hands. They are kept out of the sun and other harsh light in acid-free, temperature-controlled spaces. Other old quilts have been left in family attics, donated to thrift shops, or relegated to dog beds or rags. We hope that after recognizing the beauty of these quilts, you will come to value and care for them carefully.

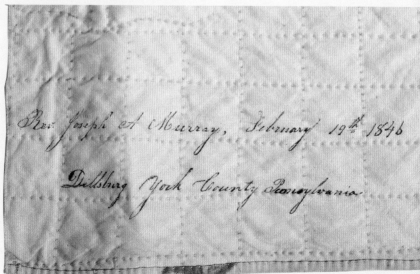

Finding and Documenting

Once you start looking, quilts are everywhere. A good place to start is with your own family. Quilts are often hidden in old trunks, blanket chests, and other long-forgotten storage places, and once they are discovered it can be a great way to learn more of your family history. Quilts also are sold at auctions, antique stores, thrift shops, and yard sales, and prices don't always reflect a quilt's value.

Triangles, c. 1930, 86.5" × 68". Made by Maud Brubaker. *Courtesy of Karen Kapp, Documentation No. MV0312*

Label with quilt information, including family history, has been sewn to the back. Permanent markers made especially for use on a cotton fabric provide the option to create beautiful and lasting documentation of a quilt's basic information.

Pieced by Maud Brubaker
Farm lady from
Ashland County, Ohio,
in the 1910's, 20's, and early 30's
Grandmother of Ruth and JoAnne
Brubaker and Lona Climenhaga of
Messiah Village, Mechanicsburg, Pa.
Quilted by Barbara Heshey, friend and
neighbor of Maud's. Barbara was a
second grandmother to the girls who
always had pinwheel cookies in the slant
topped jar on the kitchen counter.

After acquiring a quilt, the first step is to do some detective and documentation work. Write down where and when you found it, including any other bits of history you can find–even if the accuracy is questionable. Check the quilt itself for labels, names, dates, and anything that identifies it. Take good photos of your quilt and keep all of the documentation with it. A cotton bag is a good, safe storage place for the accompanying documents.

Treat your quilt with care and respect. Just by claiming it, you have done something important. If you want to do more, research its age, style, and value. The References section offer some sources (see Aug 2002 and 2004, Brackman 1989 and 1993, and Ryan 2000). Appraisers can be found in most communities, and often a quilt guild or other textile group can help.

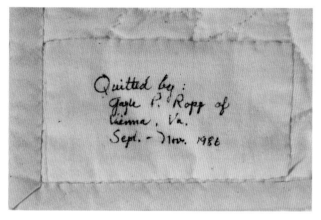
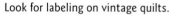
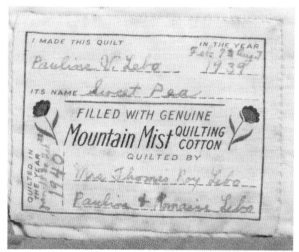

Look for labeling on vintage quilts.

Cleaning

One of the first questions people ask is how to clean old quilts. They often smell bad, have stains and dirt on them, and just beg to be thrown in the washing machine! Please resist that urge, at least initially. While it is true that dirt and mildew are hard on the fibers, cleaning may potentially be worse. Museums and purists never wash quilts. Some quilts are better off with a thorough washing, however, and many quilts you find will have been carelessly washed many times. However, following these simple guidelines will keep your quilt looking its best.

Quilts can be safely aired out. The best way to do this is to place it outside on a dry, sunny day, sandwiched between cotton sheets to let the fresh air do its work. Direct sunlight can seriously fade fabrics, so be sure to cover your quilt and lay it flat to protect the fibers.

Strippy Medallion, first half made in the 1900s, 77" × 84". Maker unknown. This quilt was completed in stages. The design fabrics date to the early 1900s and were pieced onto newpaper for stabilizing in the 1950s. The borders are also from several time periods. When completing unfinished blocks, it is often more aesthetically pleasing to maintain consistency in the style or time frame of fabrics, though artistic interpretation may lead to other decisions. *Courtesy of Sandy Harmon, Documentation No. BV0865*

After acquiring a quilt, the first step is to do some detective and documentation work. Write down where and when you found it, including any other bits of history you can find–even if the accuracy is questionable. Check the quilt itself for labels, names, dates, and anything that identifies it. Take good photos of your quilt and keep all of the documentation with it. A cotton bag is a good, safe storage place for the accompanying documents.

Treat your quilt with care and respect. Just by claiming it, you have done something important. If you want to do more, research its age, style, and value. The References section offer some sources (see Aug 2002 and 2004, Brackman 1989 and 1993, and Ryan 2000). Appraisers can be found in most communities, and often a quilt guild or other textile group can help.

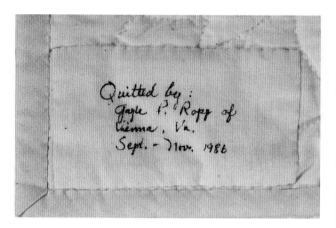
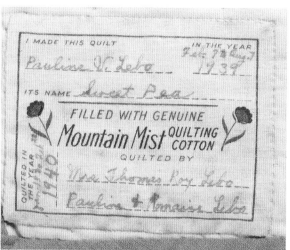

Look for labeling on vintage quilts.

Cleaning

One of the first questions people ask is how to clean old quilts. They often smell bad, have stains and dirt on them, and just beg to be thrown in the washing machine! Please resist that urge, at least initially. While it is true that dirt and mildew are hard on the fibers, cleaning may potentially be worse. Museums and purists never wash quilts. Some quilts are better off with a thorough washing, however, and many quilts you find will have been carelessly washed many times. However, following these simple guidelines will keep your quilt looking its best.

Quilts can be safely aired out. The best way to do this is to place it outside on a dry, sunny day, sandwiched between cotton sheets to let the fresh air do its work. Direct sunlight can seriously fade fabrics, so be sure to cover your quilt and lay it flat to protect the fibers.

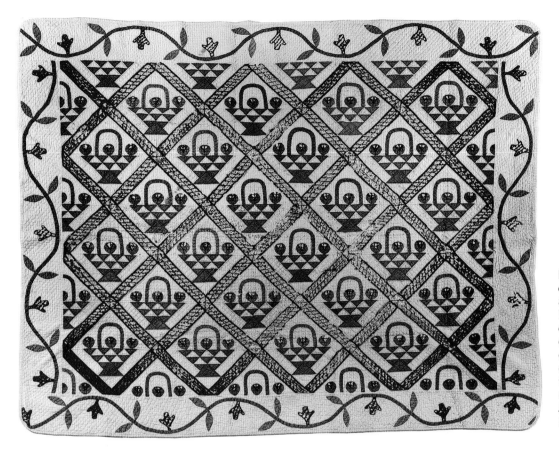

Flower Basket with Buds, c. 1870, 66.375" × 82.5". Maker unknown. Not all fabrics hold up over time. Washing and other factors may have contributed to the disintegration of most of the pink fabric in this quilt. *Courtesy of Andrea Sheya, Documentation No. TM0784*

Careful vacuuming also gets rid of dust and dirt. Use a gentle setting and put a nylon stocking or other cover over the nozzle to gently clean the soiled areas.

Washing is certainly an option for some quilts. After confirming that you aren't about to destroy an invaluable historic item, you still want to be careful. Don't use detergent; gentle soaps are available at quilt shops. Before you wash a whole quilt, test small sections to make sure the colors won't run. You can buy products that prevent colors from running in the laundry section of the supermarket, or from a quilt shop.

Remember that your quilt will become heavy when wet, and that puts a strain on the threads. So think twice before soaking it in the bathtub—getting it out can be difficult. Washing machine agitators are very hard on quilts, so bypass that cycle if you are using a machine. Soak, then spin on the gentle cycle.

Quilts are happier if dried flat. They can be laid on a clean sheet and gently straightened to their proper shape. Hanging them on a clothesline may be picturesque, but it is hard on the fibers and stretches them out of shape.

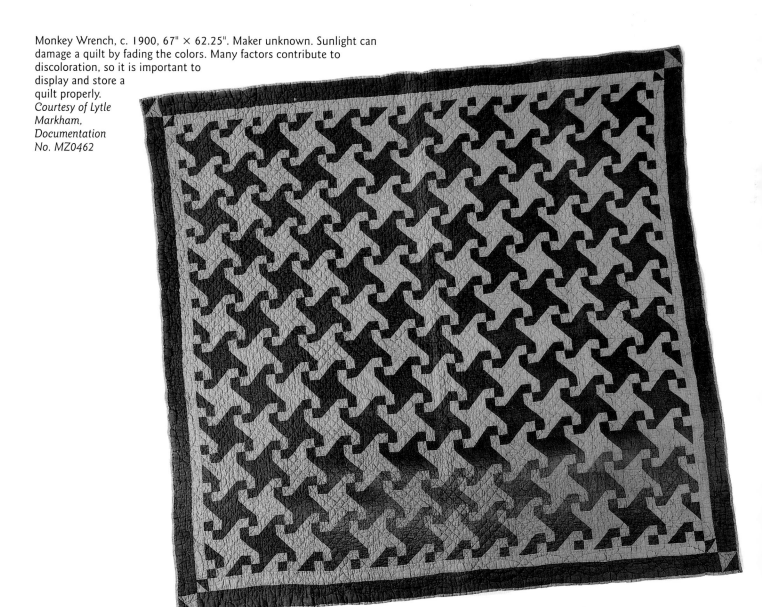

Monkey Wrench, c. 1900, 67" × 62.25". Maker unknown. Sunlight can damage a quilt by fading the colors. Many factors contribute to discoloration, so it is important to display and store a quilt properly. *Courtesy of Lytle Markham, Documentation No. MZ0462*

Conserve, Repair, Cut Up, or Finish?

Opinions differ on what to do with unfinished blocks, tops, or damaged quilts. Historians generally use minimal intervention, simply conserving it, and when needed, stabilizing fabrics to prevent further disintegration. Many quilts get repaired, and the best way to do that is with fabrics of a similar age, color, and feel as the original. Collecting fabrics of the same vintage as your quilt is an ideal way to have them on hand for mending damaged areas.

Some quilts are too far gone to save. It is not uncommon to salvage what can be saved by making it into something else—a pillow, wall-hanging, or stuffed animal. Sometimes this is the best use of an old family quilt that was loved and used for many years. What is left can be cherished and remembered.

We often find unfinished quilt blocks, partial quilt tops, or even whole tops that have never been quilted. Some quilt enthusiasts feel it is wrong to finish a partially started project. Others feel as strongly that it is a service to the original maker to complete what she or he started. If you decide to complete a project, keep in mind that a quilt is dated based on the most recent fabric and work done on it, so document what you do. Most experts recommend using similar fabrics, even vintage fabrics of the same era, when completing a previously unfinished project, and completing it in a style consistent with the original. Those who have completed a quilt out of vintage blocks or tops often feel connected to the original maker and find satisfaction in having a quilt that can be appreciated and admired.

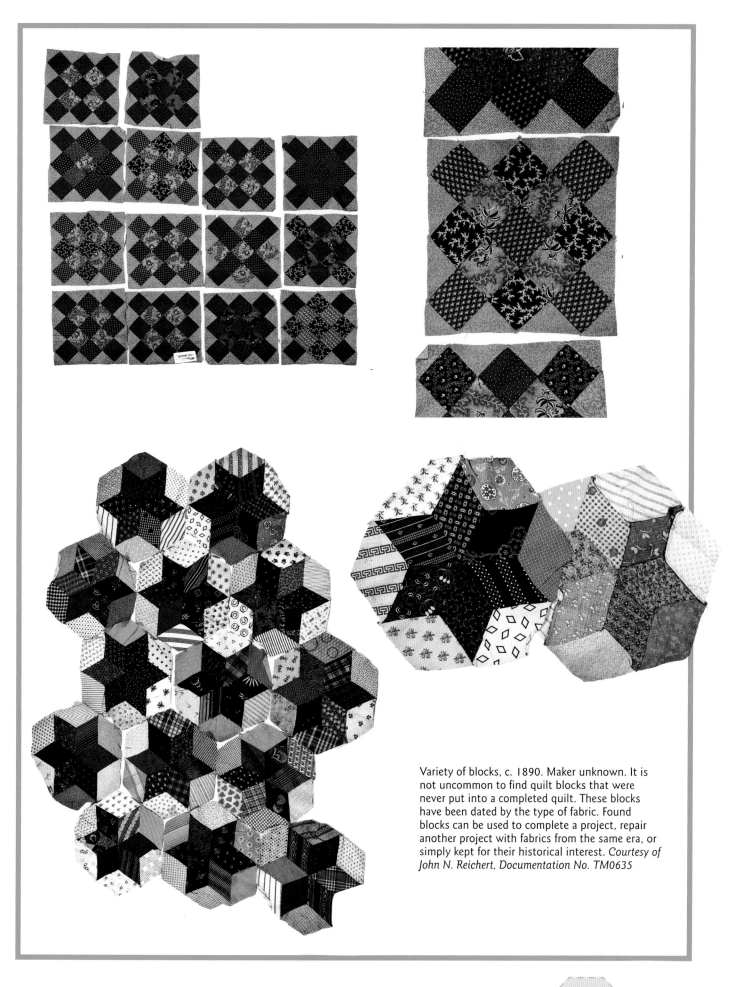

Variety of blocks, c. 1890. Maker unknown. It is not uncommon to find quilt blocks that were never put into a completed quilt. These blocks have been dated by the type of fabric. Found blocks can be used to complete a project, repair another project with fabrics from the same era, or simply kept for their historical interest. *Courtesy of John N. Reichert, Documentation No. TM0635*

Strippy Medallion, first half made in the 1900s, 77" × 84". Maker unknown. This quilt was completed in stages. The design fabrics date to the early 1900s and were pieced onto newpaper for stabilizing in the 1950s. The borders are also from several time periods. When completing unfinished blocks, it is often more aesthetically pleasing to maintain consistency in the style or time frame of fabrics, though artistic interpretation may lead to other decisions. *Courtesy of Sandy Harmon, Documentation No. BV0865*

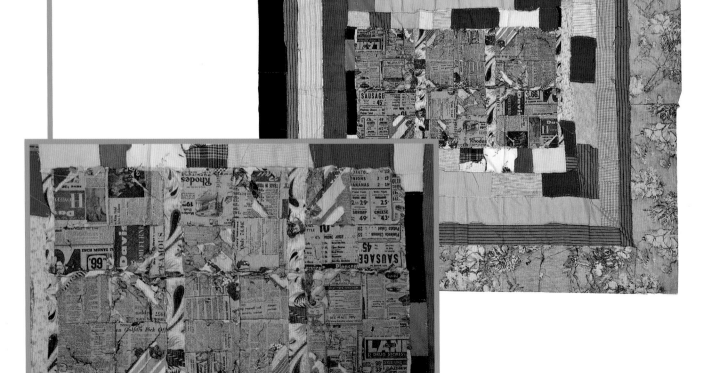

Heritage Quilt "Field Of Diamonds"
Was made by my Grandmother,
Katie F. Engle 1880-1965
About 70 years ago.
This quilt is very special to me
Because in the quilt are pieces of
Fabric from some of the dresses
I wore when I was a little child.
My Grandmother did many
Special Handcrafts,
Quilting, needlepoint, crocheting,
Braided rugs etc. she was a
Very special lady.
Jane Long

MV0318

Grandmother's Flower Garden
(Field of Diamonds), c. 1940,
93" × 83". Made by Katie
Engle. Family history with
photos helped to document
this quilt's origins. Some of its
fabrics have not held up over
the years. Small areas can be
replaced with similar fabrics,
preferably from the same
general time period. *Courtesy
of Jane Long, Documentation
No. MV0318*

Care and Storage

Once you own a quilt, the question becomes what to do with it. Museum pieces are stored and protected from things that can damage older fibers. However, if a quilt isn't seen, it can't be appreciated. Even if you opt not to use a quilt every day, consider finding a way to have it out where it can be appreciated, at least some of the time.

Quilts can be used as a wall hanging, draped over a quilt rack or other furniture, or used on beds. If you want to hang your quilt, it is a good idea to have a cloth rod pocket made and attached to the top. Curtain rods make good hangers for quilts, and you may find other hanging options. Remember that hanging can put a strain on the quilt, so rotate or rest it periodically.

If you are using a quilt on a bed or other furniture, remember that sunlight will fade it and damage the fibers. Place it in a room with low light, or at least cover the quilt where the sun hits it.

If you store your quilts, keep in mind that they are happiest in places where they can breathe and temperatures are moderate. Avoid plastic bags and boxes, and attics and basements, where conditions are hot or humid. Consider wrapping a quilt in a cotton sheet or pillowcase, or acid-free box or tissue paper. Surprisingly, blanket chests are not good storage places for quilts, as direct contact with the wood can discolor them. At least cover your quilt with a cotton bag before storing it.

Finally, there is the issue of folding. We all fold our quilts to store them. Whether using your quilt often or keeping it stored, be sure to vary the folds frequently to avoid damaging the fibers. If you have a spare bed, an ideal solution is to lay the quilts one on top of the other, covered with a clean sheet to keep out dust and light.

Double Irish Chain, c. 1880, 85" × 81". Maker unknown. When storing quilts, refold them periodically to reduce the wear on fold lines. Quilts can be safely stored in acid-free boxes or cotton bags and should be refolded or rolled frequently. *Courtesy of Joseph and Karen Buckley, Documentation No. KB0417*

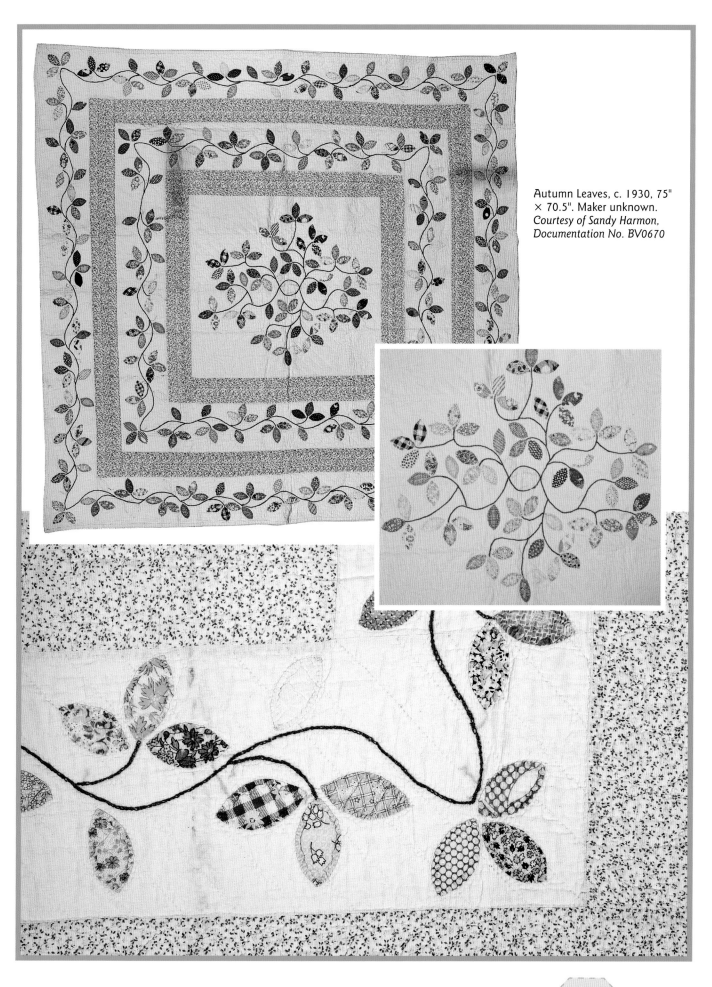

Autumn Leaves, c. 1930, 75"
× 70.5". Maker unknown.
*Courtesy of Sandy Harmon,
Documentation No. BV0670*

We hope this book has piqued your interest in and respect for this beautiful work done (mostly) by women over the past several hundred years. The Cumberland County documentation project showed us that quilts move around a lot – perhaps now more than ever. It is our hope that some of those quilts will find homes where they are cherished and valued, whether they return to their place of origin or reside a world away from their roots.

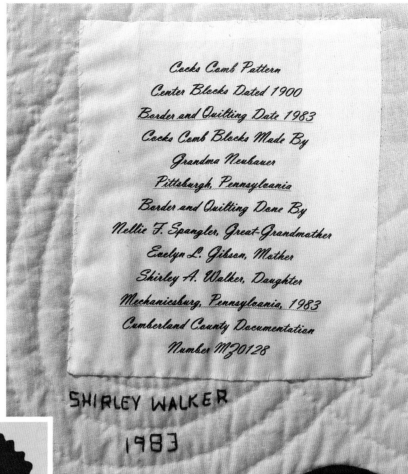

Coxcomb, blocks, c.1900, quilt finished 1983, 83" × 83". Current owner recalls, "The center was made by Grandma Neubauer on my father's side. My mother and grandmother on my mother's side and I marked the quilt with Grandma's cardboard patterns and quilted it on a rolling frame. We marked it with pencil—this was my learning how to do quilts and it was the old way." Making a quilt from previously unfinished blocks can create a family heirloom that is more appreciated than plain blocks. This quilt, worked on by three generations in one family, contains many memories that have been documented and will stay with the quilt. *Courtesy of Shirley A. Walker, Documentation No. MZ0128*

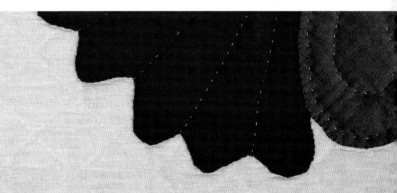

Duck and Ducklings variation, c. 1930. Maker unknown. This lovely quilt was obviously made with great care and skill. The pieced blocks form a simple and finely crafted pattern. Feathered circles are quilted in the white areas, and the word "Mother" has been written with quilt stitches. There was no way to identify who made it, or who it was made for. *Courtesy of Sandy Harmon, Documentation No. BV0852*

References

Adams County Quilt Project. *The Hands that Made Them: Quilts of Adams County, Pennsylvania*. Camp Hill, PA: Adams County Quilt Project, 1993.

Allen, Gloria S. and Nancy G. Tuckhorn. *A Maryland Album; Quiltmaking Traditions–1634–1934*. Nashville, TN: Rutledge Hill Press, 1995.

Arkansas Quilter's Guild. *Arkansas Quilts*. Padukah, KY: American Quilter's Society, 1984.

Aug, Bobbi A., Sharon Newman and Gerald Roy. *Vintage Quilts; Identifying, Collecting, Dating, Preserving and Valuing*. Paduka, KY: Collector Books, A Division of Schroeder Publishing, 2002.

Aug, Bobbi A. and Gerald Roy. *Antique Quilts and Textiles: A Price Guide to Functional and Fashionable Cloth Comforts*. Padukah, KY: Collector Books, A Division of Schroeder Publishing, 2004.

Bell, Raymond M. *Mother Cumberland*. Carlisle, PA: Hearthside Press, 1989.

Bell, Whitfield J., A. B., A. M., PhD. "Substance of Remarks on the History of Cumberland County, Notes on the Bicentennial." Cumberland County, PA, June 19, 1951 Baranowski, Willa. *Historical Penny Squares Embroidery Patterns*. Paducah, KY: American Quilter's Society, 1996.

Brackman, Barbara. *Clues in the Calico: A Guide to Identifying and Dating Antique Quilts*. McLean, VA: EPM Publications, 1989.

Brackman, Barbara. *Encyclopedia of Pieced Quilt Patterns*. Padukah, KY: American Quilter's Society, 1993.

Burdick, Nancilu B. *Family Ties: Old Quilt Patterns from New Cloth*. Nashville, TN: Rutledge Hill Press, 1991.

Cawley, Lucinda R., Lorraine D. Ezbiansky and Denise R. Nordberg. *Saved for the People of Pennsylvania; Quilts from the State Museum of Pennsylvania*. Harrisburg, PA: Pennsylvania Historical and Museum Commission, 1997.

Chester County Historical Society. *Layers: Unfolding the Stories of Chester County Quilts*. Chester County, PA: The Chester County Historical Society, 2009.

Connecticut Quilt Search Project. *Quilts and Quiltmakers Covering Connecticut*. Atglen, PA: Schiffer Publishing, 2002.

Cumberland County Visitor's Guide, 2003.

Flower, Milton E. *Cumberland County, Pennsylvania 1750–1951*. Carlisle, PA: Cumberland County Commissioners, 1995.

Flower, Milton E. "A History of Cumberland County," *Book of the Centuries: Commemorating the Two Hundredth Anniversary of Carlisle and Cumberland County, PA.* Carlisle, PA, 1951.

Herr, Patricia T. *Quilting Traditions: Pieces from the Past.* Atglen, PA: Schiffer Publishing, 2000.

Hersh, Charles and Tandy. *Cloth and Costume 1750 to 1800: Cumberland County, Pennsylvania.* Camp Hill, PA: Cumberland County Historical Society Plank Suburban Press, 1995.

Ryan, Roslea, ed. *Collecting Quilts with Narelle Grieve.* Sydney, Australia: Express Publications, 2000.

Valentine, Fawn. *West Virginia Quilts and Quiltmakers: Echoes from the Hills.* Athens, OH: Ohio University Press, 2000.

Virginia Consortium of Quilters. *Quilts of Virginia 1607–1899: The Birth of America Through the Eye of a Needle.* Atglen, PA: Schiffer Publishing, 2006.

Wallace, Paul A. W. *Indian Paths of Pennsylvania.* Harrisburg, PA: Pennsylvania Historical and Museum Commission, 1965.

Weinraub, Anita Z. ed. *Georgia Quilts: Piecing Together A History.* Athens, GA: The University of Georgia Press, 2006.

York County Quilt Documentation Project and the York County Heritage Trust. *Quilts; The Fabric of Friendship.* Atglen, PA: Schiffer Publishing, 2000.